Reverse

Diablo II

Reverse Design Series

Author

Patrick Holleman

Series Titles

Reverse Design
Diablo II

Patrick Holleman

CRC Press
Taylor & Francis Group
Boca Raton London New York

CRC Press is an imprint of the
Taylor & Francis Group, an **informa** business

CRC Press
Taylor & Francis Group
6000 Broken Sound Parkway NW, Suite 300
Boca Raton, FL 33487-2742

© 2019 by Taylor & Francis Group, LLC
CRC Press is an imprint of Taylor & Francis Group, an Informa business

No claim to original U.S. Government works

Printed on acid-free paper

International Standard Book Number-13: 978-1-138-32327-8 (Paperback)
978-1-138-32328-5 (Hardback)

This book contains information obtained from authentic and highly regarded sources. Reasonable efforts have been made to publish reliable data and information, but the author and publisher cannot assume responsibility for the validity of all materials or the consequences of their use. The authors and publishers have attempted to trace the copyright holders of all material reproduced in this publication and apologize to copyright holders if permission to publish in this form has not been obtained. If any copyright material has not been acknowledged, please write and let us know so we may rectify in any future reprint.

Except as permitted under U.S. Copyright Law, no part of this book may be reprinted, reproduced, transmitted, or utilized in any form by any electronic, mechanical, or other means, now known or hereafter invented, including photocopying, microfilming, and recording, or in any information storage or retrieval system, without written permission from the publishers.

For permission to photocopy or use material electronically from this work, please access www.copyright.com (http://www.copyright.com/) or contact the Copyright Clearance Center, Inc. (CCC), 222 Rosewood Drive, Danvers, MA 01923, 978-750-8400. CCC is a not-for-profit organization that provides licenses and registration for a variety of users. For organizations that have been granted a photocopy license by the CCC, a separate system of payment has been arranged.

Trademark Notice: Product or corporate names may be trademarks or registered trademarks, and are used only for identification and explanation without intent to infringe.

Library of Congress Cataloging-in-Publication Data

Names: Holleman, Patrick, author.
Title: Reverse design. Diablo II / Patrick Holleman.
Other titles: Diablo II | Diable Two
Description: Boca Raton, FL : CRC Press/Taylor & Francis Group, 2018.
Identifiers: LCCN 2018018873| ISBN 9781138323278 (pbk. : acid-free paper) |
ISBN 9781138323285 (hardback : acid-free paper)
Subjects: LCSH: Video games--Design. | Fantasy games--Design.
Classification: LCC GV1469.3 .H66 2018 | DDC 794.8--dc23
LC record available at https://lccn.loc.gov/2018018873

Visit the Taylor & Francis Web site at
http://www.taylorandfrancis.com

and the CRC Press Web site at
http://www.crcpress.com

Contents

Introduction

This is the sixth book in the *Reverse Design* series and the final book in Volume One. The goal of the series has been to reverse-engineer all of the design decisions that went into classic videogames. Other books in this series include entries on *Final Fantasy VI*, *Chrono Trigger*, *Super Mario World*, *Half-Life*, and *Final Fantasy VII*. You do not need to have read those books in order to understand this one, although the *Final Fantasy VII* book provides some excellent context for the kinds of historical design trends that created both it and *Diablo II*. This book is, nevertheless, a bit different from the previous books. For one thing, it is shorter than the previous three books (which were all around 50,000 words, while this one is closer to 40,000). One of the reasons for this is that *Diablo II* is almost entirely made up of systems rather than content. That is, *Diablo II* does not have bespoke levels in the same way that *Super Mario World* has levels. In *Super Mario World*, every single thing that appears in every level of the game was placed there by the hand of a level designer. The levels in *Diablo II*, on the other hand, are (mostly) created by an algorithm. So, instead of having to describe 70 levels, this book has to describe the algorithms that make *Diablo II's* levels. Those algorithms are complex, but describing a few algorithms is a shorter task than describing several dozen levels, no matter how complex those algorithms are.

The other way in which this book is different is the amount and type of information I had access to while writing it. Of the five books written before this one, four of them were about Japanese games. My Japanese is only conversational, and I have no contacts in the Japanese gaming industry. Beyond that, Japanese developers are a little more reluctant than Western game developers to talk about their creative process in a highly detailed way. Thus, most of the information I had about the development of these games came from commercial interviews or fan-made walkthroughs. The interviews are occasionally useful, but rarely thorough. The walkthroughs are often astonishingly informative, thorough and well-organized, and without them I could not have written the books, but neither of those resources is as direct as a developer sitting down and telling you his or her intent. For this book, I interviewed four of the central figures in *Diablo II's* development: project leads Max Schaefer and David Brevik, lead designer Stieg Hedlund, and level designer Stefan Scandizzo. The information that they provided gave me the ability to measure their intentions against their results—something that I couldn't really do in the other books in this series.

The final way in which this book is different from the others in the series is that, even if you have played *Diablo II*, you may not have played the game that I am writing about. In the age of DLC, everyone is familiar with the notion of an expanding game. *Diablo II* has more DLC than most people realize, however. In addition to the massive expansion that happened in *Lord of Destruction* (2001), the game has been slowly revised and enlarged consistently since its release. Thus, anyone who stopped playing in 2000, or 2002, or even 2006 would find that the game has changed significantly since then. The version of the game that I will be writing about is a variant of 1.13, which is the last version that I could play in a live multiplayer environment. There is a certain amount of conflict between my use of this version and my use of interviews with the game's original creators. None of the four developers that I interviewed had anything to do with the game after 2004. Nevertheless, I have not found anything in the design that contradicts the original principles laid down by the primary contributors to the game.

The Structure of this Book

This book breaks down into three large chapters, and each chapter breaks down into several smaller sections. Chapter 1 deals with the historical lineage of *Diablo II*, examining how a combination of existing action games and RPGs led to the game which we know today. Chapter 2 examines the different kinds of randomness that appear in the game and affect the algorithms that generate things like maps, enemy affixes, and loot drops. (I use the term affixes a lot in this document. It is a *Diablo*-specific term for any procedurally-added change in monster or item stats or abilities.) Chapter 3 synthesizes the former two sections and examines the way that procedural generation techniques replicate the fundamental design structure of action games, but in an RPG context, in a phenomenon I call Schaefer variation. Chapter 3 also looks at how Schaefer variation naturally leads to an RPG-specific psychological phenomenon I call acceleration flow. Because these three parts can be useful on their own, I have given a slightly larger summary of each part just below.

The first step in understanding *Diablo II* is to understand it in its historical context. *Diablo II* is an unusual RPG in that it is the product of three convergent trends in the field of game design. Those trends are the combination strategy, the specialization strategy, and the prevalence of Nishikado motion. These are a lot of technical terms, and you don't need to understand them yet. We'll examine each of those ideas in turn, but the short version of the story is that *Diablo II* borrows from roguelikes, action RPGs, and console videogames in roughly equal measure. *Diablo II* isn't unique in making this combination; lots of other games use some or all of these same elements. The specific way in which those things come together in *Diablo II* is systematically elegant in a way that few games are. In the first section of this book, I'm going to examine the historical origins of each of *Diablo II's* design ideas, and see how *Diablo II* took them in a new direction. Specifically, we'll look at how *Diablo II* borrows selectively—and in many cases, partially—from the roguelike genre. We'll also look at how *Diablo II* supplements certain parts of the roguelike genre with design ideas from traditional RPGs (like character classes) and console action games. Chapter 1 is mostly specific to *Diablo II* and examines how the design ideas and balance structures in *Diablo II* compare to the analogous parts of the game's ancestors.

Chapter 2 of this book examines the various forms of randomness that appear in *Diablo II*. *Diablo II* is a great example of several different ways that randomness can be used in videogame design. *Diablo II* is known for its procedurally-generated maps and procedurally-dropped loot. Descriptions of *Diablo II* often use the term "random" to describe both systems. To some degree, that's correct; both systems do use random selections as their primary means of generation, but both systems are also very different from one another, and from players' expectations of them, especially in the ways that they place constraints on their randomness. The best way to understand the map generation algorithm and all its constraints is to see the algorithm as a person playing a card game. The best way to understand the item generation system is to see items as slices of pie—unless you're trying to understand the odds of finishing a set of items. It's best to understand the randomness of set items as being like a game of *Scrabble*. There are also more straightforward forms of probability which govern some of the game's systems. What's more, many of these systems interact with one another! Accordingly, the entirety of Chapter 2 of this document is dedicated to unpacking the various ways that randomness and procedural generation (not always the same thing in *Diablo II*) are used. Chapter 2 contains lessons that are widely applicable, not just to RPGs, but to any game in which procedural generation and randomness play a significant role.

Chapter 3 of this document examines a phenomenon I call Schaefer variation. If there is a central thesis to this book, it is that Schaefer variation is the defining design feature of *Diablo II*. The quickest way to explain Schaefer variation is to say that it is a way of using procedural generation to emulate the kind of difficulty curves found in console action games. The defining moment in the history of videogames was the serendipitous discovery of its central design structure, Nishikado motion (which is defined in Chapter 1 of this book). In *Diablo II*, the designers figured out a way of recreating the up-and-down action of Nishikado motion in a procedural context. That recreation is Schafer variation. Although Schaefer variation's primary effect is to emulate the central design dynamic of action games, it also has an effect which is idiosyncratic to RPGs. Because the difficulty of RPGs is inherently tied to the level up system, the up-and-down motion caused by Schaefer variation also results in a phenomenon called acceleration flow. We'll take a look at what that phenomenon is, how it happens, and how it affects the player's experience of *Diablo II*. Chapter 3 is the most theoretical section of this book, and the one most specific to RPGs with long level-up systems and tons of gear.

The Different Kinds of RPG, and How *Diablo II* Borrows from Them

The Original Problem of Digitial RPGs

From an academic perspective, the best thing about RPG history is that it has a clear beginning. The first RPG was definitely one of the early forms of *Dungeons & Dragons* (hereafter *D&D* except at the beginning of a sentence), which were developed from 1968 through 1970. The development of *D&D* explains why there are so many different kinds of RPGs today, and why the audience for one type might not like another. In the previous book in this series, *Reverse Design: Final Fantasy VII*, I laid out a fairly comprehensive history of the path from *D&D* to modern RPGs. If you're looking for a longer explanation of RPG design history, I recommend that book and the many great books it cites, especially the work of Jon Peterson and Shannon Appelcline. For this book, however, we only need to look at two events that happened relatively early in the history of RPGs: the birth of the specialization style and the birth of the action RPG. These two events occurred in reaction to *D&D* and created the majority of the design material that would eventually make up *Diablo II*.

  Dungeons & Dragons presents a huge problem for RPG designers: it does almost everything that an RPG can do. By the early 1980s, *D&D* already included hundreds (if not thousands) of important RPG design ideas, and these were not small ideas, either. Most of the structural systems which we would recognize in our modern RPGs had already seen a few iterations by the time the books comprising *Advanced D&D* (*AD&D*) came out. Ideas like random enemy spawns, randomized loot, lighting levels in dungeons, ability cooldowns, difficulty settings, and item creation all existed in *D&D* long before any videogame designer attempted to use them.[1–3] The staggering completeness of *D&D* meant that designers had a hard time making an RPG that felt mechanically original. Many of the first RPGs to emulate *D&D* only changed the setting and aesthetics. There are many games that are more or less *D&D* in space, or in steampunk settings, etc. Some of those games are classics, but they didn't really change the scope or methods of the RPG genre. One game took the opposite strategy, however, and focused only on a small subset of *D&D*'s mechanics. That game was *Rogue*, which spawned the roguelike genre.

Rogue abandons all the parts of an RPG that do not directly relate to dungeon crawling. There are no towns, there is essentially no plot, and there are no mini-games or dialogue trees. There is only dungeon crawling. The goal of *Rogue* is to get a player into a dungeon as fast as possible, and keep him or her there indefinitely—always crawling more dungeon. *Rogue* doesn't have any features that were not, in some form, originally invented in *D&D*. Yet, *Rogue* seems very different from its source material because it focuses so intently on doing one thing. *Rogue* can kill the player character more often than the average *D&D* campaign because the player is back in the dungeon after a few button presses. Moreover, *Rogue* can force the player to learn all the tricks of its dungeons in a short period of time because there aren't that many tricks. The player doesn't have to worry about party composition and job classes. *Rogue* is also able to have a greater degree of volatility in its random operations because the game is too short for any single game event to have far-reaching effects. The player can never really lose more than a few hours of progress. These tradeoffs are the secret to the success of *Rogue*, and all games that use the same design strategy. *Rogue* gets rid of certain RPG design ideas to embellish others. This design strategy is what I call *specialization*. A specialization-type RPG is any RPG that focuses on just a tiny part of the *D&D* source material. In spawning the roguelike genre, *Rogue* made a template for a certain kind of specialization that the *Diablo* designers would eventually use.

There are two design ideas that are embellished in historically important ways in *Rogue*. The first idea is procedural content generation, and the second idea is permadeath. Procedural content generation means that some parts of a game's content, like level layouts, monster stats, and magical item properties are created by an algorithm rather than by the direct work of a designer. Rogue relies very heavily on procedural content generation. Procedural content allows for an effectively infinite variety of dungeons to explore, which is necessary for *Rogue* since there's nothing else to do in the game. *Dungeons & Dragons* actually pioneered procedural content generation, although it relied on dice and the human imagination to implement it. Room layouts, item drops, and enemy encounters in *D&D* are often augmented by (paper) procedures. *Rogue* simply goes further than *D&D* does by making nearly every aspect of the game design procedural. Permadeath, on the other hand, requires that with every death of the player character, the game starts over from scratch, with nothing preserved. This makes *Rogue* longer by forcing the player to play fresh dungeons every time he or she dies. For arcade games of the 1980s, this is a common enough strategy for extending the life of a game's content. For RPGs, with their focus on long-term character progression, this is not especially common. Parties in *D&D* campaigns are, of course, wiped out all the time, but *Rogue* embellishes this idea by making it more common, and by eliminating most of the player's defenses against it. Few dungeon masters kill their players' parties multiple times an hour, but in *Rogue*, this would not be surprising at all.

As an important historical aside, I want to point out that while the key embellishments in *Rogue* were a product of an artistic reaction against *D&D*, the game was also shaped by technological concerns. No commercial computer in 1981 could have simulated all of the major systems in *D&D*. *Rogue* saves time by abandoning a large amount of the standard *D&D* systems. *Rogue* goes further, however, in that it also abandons content in favor of algorithms. The tabletop RPG lives on content. That is, a designer (such as your group's dungeon master) creates and/or deploys a series of pre-constructed encounters which add up to a campaign. *Rogue's* designers turned this content generation almost entirely over to a set of algorithms that construct dungeons, place monsters, and dispense items. This lack of content saves a lot of disc space, which, in 1981, was a precious resource. It also saves the design team a lot of time and money spent on making content. The next section looks at how, as technology and time constraints loosened, later roguelikes and derivative subgenres preserved the primacy of procedural content even when they didn't have to. Eventually, a technological constraint became an artistic constraint, and the roguelike became an ingredient in other kinds of RPGs.

Roguelikeness as a Commodity

The oldest theme in the history of videogame design is that technological constraints become artistic strategies. Tomohiro Nishikado (whom we will discuss again later) turned an unexpected property of a microprocessor into the foundation of all mainstream videogame design. In a similar fashion, the designers of *Diablo II* took procedural generation and permadeath (two ideas instituted partly because of technical constraints) as they appear in *Rogue* and roguelikes and turned them into artistic resources. One of the most important things to know about *Diablo II* is that it plays with its source material and implements it in an idiosyncratic way. In essence, the designers of *Diablo II* saw that roguelikeness was not a binary thing; games can be somewhat roguelike. The most obvious example of this is the fact that the *Diablo* games take place in real time, whereas most of its roguelike predecessors are turn-based. There are plenty of other examples, however. Player death in *Diablo II* is clearly based on its roguelike antecedents, but with some adaptations for a wider audience. When a player-character dies (on softcore setting), that character loses gold and experience points. Some of that can be retrieved if the player can reach his or her own corpse, but some of it is irretrievable. Thus, death is penalized—sometimes quite heavily—but in a way that's more appropriate for a mainstream audience. Then again, *Diablo II* also has a hardcore setting which reinstitutes permadeath if the player wants the extra challenge. Procedural generation is also something the designers play with rather than employ entirely. Traditional roguelike dungeons are almost entirely algorithmic, whereas many locations in *Diablo II* actually have a great deal of fixed terrain and fixed enemy locations—far more than most people imagine.[4]

Some of the ways in which *Diablo II* deviates from the roguelike formula are actually very informative about the degree to which the designers wanted to recapture the old roguelike spirit. In early roguelikes, item identification is an important bottleneck that prevents players from being able to use just any item they find. Not only are many items unidentified when the player picks them up, but the item identification scroll itself is an unidentified item that needs to be used blindly in order to determine what it is. This kind of volatility and blind chance was one of the things that David Brevik said he liked about early roguelikes, but which didn't fit the voice of the *Diablo* games.[5] Indeed, not only was that kind of blind volatility diminished, it was actually reversed in some of the game's mechanics. In *Diablo II*, Deckard Cain can mass-identify an entire inventory's worth of items.

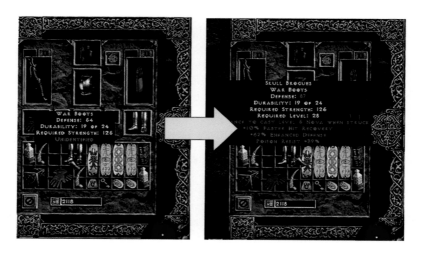

It would be easy to see this change as modern developers dumbing down their product to reach casual players. This is an assumption game critics have made for as long as there have been identifiable videogame genres. But, like many RPGs of its time, *Diablo II* is actually dropping one idea to embellish another. They wanted to widen their audience, yes, but they also wanted to speed up and expand the game.

By eliminating the identification bottleneck, *Diablo II* is able to center the game's focus on the item acquisition loop. There was nothing accidental about this. Brevik wanted to recapture the experience of playing Angband and Moria, two roguelikes he enjoyed in college. He remembered that he and several friends would play in the computer lab together (even though these were single-player games), and they would shout to one another to come and look when a rare and powerful item would drop. "You basically never actually killed the balrog," he said. "You would play for those really rare items instead."[6] Max Schaefer said something similar, saying that his focus was in creating powerful items that allowed players to have differing experiences of the game.[7] Although permadeath and other roguelike design ideas were important to the designers, the primary experience that they wanted to recreate was the ecstatic discovery of a very rare item that caused a sudden swing in difficulty.

The Legacy of the Tabletop: Character Classes

Another way that *Diablo II* diverges from its roguelike ancestors is in the use of character classes. Although the character class was one of the foundational ideas of the RPG, the roguelikes from which *Diablo II* borrows many of its core ideas did not use character classes in a significant way. This was probably a product of their idiosyncratic reduction in scope. *Diablo II*, despite having a comparatively massive budget, mostly sticks to the reduced scope that it inherited from the roguelike. Real-time gameplay doesn't really take *Diablo II* away from the volatility, danger and endless (but narrow) variation of the roguelike, it just recasts those things in real time. Character classes, however, are a major deviation from the roguelikes that directly inspired the game. Every character class feels distinct, and their differences are reflected in the underlying systems of the game. Below is a graph that visualizes the primary statistical difference (HP) between classes in *Diablo II*.[8]

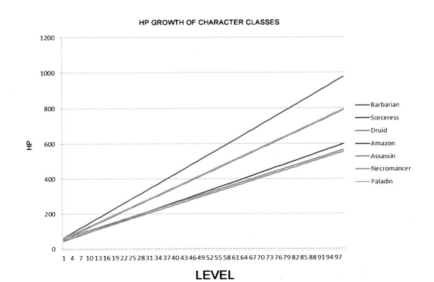

Although the most obvious trend is the divide between fragile casters and hearty melee fighters, the classes exist on a spectrum rather than in two undifferentiated lumps. There are quite a few differences between classes, although we're only going to examine the statistical parts in this section. In the next section of this book, we will also examine the action-game differences between classes, like differences in mobility and crowd control skills. For now, we're going to focus on simulated skill systems (RPG stats) and the few class-based items the game employs.

Historically, character classes in Western RPGs have been distinguished by the abilities they possess and the gear they equip. *Diablo* adheres to the former criterion, but not the latter. Each class features distinct abilities, especially in their passives. When it comes to gear, *Diablo II* experiments with a small amount of class-based gear, but most of it is usable by any class. In this section, we're going to primarily examine how character abilities distinguish each character class, and how that is a product of the traditional tabletop RPGs that influenced its designers. Most of this section will be about traditional RPG abilities and the RPG systems that support them. Although the character classes of *Diablo II* resemble their tabletop antecedents in many ways, there's a big difference beneath the surface. In tabletop RPGs, some characters hardly deal any damage to enemies at all. Instead, they heal, protect, enhance, obscure, redirect, negotiate, and do many other things. In *Diablo II*, all characters are constructed to slay hordes of enemies. Barbarians and Paladins are much better at tanking than Sorceresses and Necromancers, but they have to be able to slaughter the demonic hordes by themselves, or else *Diablo* loses its unique voice. This is one of the primary reasons why this book contains so little about multiplayer mechanics. As more players join a *Diablo II* game, the HP, experience values, and item drop rates increase in a way that's very favorable to the player, encouraging large parties. However, there are no statistical changes to enemies that would require the tank/DPS/heal balance. A team of eight Sorceresses will perform just as well as a more balanced team, and that's intentional.

Character Systems Overview

Before we get to each class, I want to unpack some of the systems that those classes share. There are three different dynamics that differentiate character classes: base stats, elemental availability, and mobility skills. Base stats are the numbers that make all of *Diablo II's* simulated skills work. Base stats are things like strength, dexterity, energy, and vitality. These stats give characters physical damage and carrying capacity, hit rating and evasion, mana and HP, and a few other benefits besides. Every time a character gains a level, the player can invest five points into one of these base stats, but depending on character class, the benefits will be different. The player also invests in the base stats of skills, putting points into offensive spells, mobility skills, and passive abilities to raise their effectiveness. These too differ greatly between classes—and sometimes even differ greatly between different builds of the same class. Finally, each class has a unique elemental profile. That is, each class has access to a few types of damage, but no class has access to all the types.

Base Stats

Like all RPGs, *Diablo II* is built on a system of simulated skills. A simulated skill is any skill that a character learns, rather than the player who controls that character. In *Mortal Kombat*, for example, the player has to learn and perform a button combination in order to use a fireball attack. In *Diablo II*, the Sorceress can learn the fireball attack at level twelve if the player chooses it. After that, the player only has to point and click. Because *Diablo II* is an action game, there's some skill in aiming the fireball and other skills like it, but making the fireball more powerful is mostly a matter of stats rather than skill. (There are a small number of skills that really benefit from action mechanics, but we'll get to them in the next section.) Fortunately, *Diablo II* offers quite a few different ways to augment the basic stats of a character or character's skill, which is why these stats merit their own section.

Vitality and Energy

The most basic form of simulated skill in *Diablo II* is the stat point. Most RPGs have stat points that a player can invest in a character, either by random chance or out of a budget. *Diablo II* gives the player points to invest out of a budget earned after a character gains a level. Most of its stats closely resemble those that were originally invented in *D&D* with a few minor differences. For example, the vitality stat in *Diablo II* closely resembles the constitution stat from *D&D*. Investing points into either stat will allow the character to gain more HP. The exact implementation is different—points invested in vitality directly affect HP in *Diablo II*, whereas in *D&D*, there is also some randomness in the process. The fundamental idea is, however, very similar. Energy does for spell resources (the mana pool) what vitality does for HP. The *Diablo II* energy stat doesn't have a great analogue in *D&D* for this reason. In *D&D*, the character has to rest for a certain amount of time before replenishing his skills. In *Diablo II*, the player has to use a potion or a skill that regenerates points. Also, energy stat has no effect on the power of spells. This is relatively rare—even in games that allow direct investment of points into skills, there is usually a separate character stat which also contributes to the power of some spells. In *Diablo II*, this is only true of skills with a physical component. Spells in *Diablo II* only gain power from skill-specific points.

Strength and Dexterity

Strength and dexterity in *Diablo II* are also close to their *D&D*/roguelike ancestors, with one small change that has some huge consequences. Strength allows characters to wield heavier armor and heavier weapons, and to deal more damage with melee attacks. All of that is totally orthodox RPG design. Dexterity plays a huge role in hit rate for physical attacks—both melee and ranged attacks. This is also orthodox to the tabletop games that existed at the time of *Diablo II*'s release. The only real deviation from contemporary tabletop stats is that dexterity also governs ranged damage. We'll cover this in more depth in the section on hit rates, but the basic idea is that dexterity is twice as useful for ranged attackers as strength is for melee fighters. Not only does dexterity help their damage, it also makes their attacks more accurate at the same time. Because ranged attackers get to "double dip" in dexterity, many ranged attacks are balanced (one might say penalized) in a way that melee attacks are not. In theory, this is a perfectly acceptable tradeoff, but in execution there are some oversights. We'll examine those abilities in the character sections, but it does seem like the genesis of this problem is the fact that ranged attackers get two bonuses.

The only really unorthodox dynamic in the implementation of stats in *Diablo II* is the way that stat points confer different amounts of benefit for different characters. In most RPGs, a single point in any given stat confers the same amount of general benefit, regardless of class. There may be class-based abilities that apply higher or lower multipliers to those stats, but basic rolls depending on a stat like wisdom or charisma will be the same for any two character classes who have the same value in that stat and no other modifiers (like feats). In *Diablo II*, the returns on HP and mana investment differ significantly across the characters. These returns are intuitive, however; the Barbarian gets twice as much HP from vitality as the Sorceress, and the reverse is true for mana and energy. The other characters are somewhere in the middle.

Dexterity, Level and Hit Rates

In *Diablo II*, magical attacks have a 100% hit rate if the spell animation comes in contact with the targeted monster's sprite. Physical attacks only hit if the player has a sufficiently high level, a sufficiently high hit rating, and a little bit of luck. The single most important determining factor in hit rates is the attacking character's hit rating, measured against the defending monster's defense rating. Below is a graph showing how increases in hit rating increase the overall chance of hitting a monster of an equal level.[9]

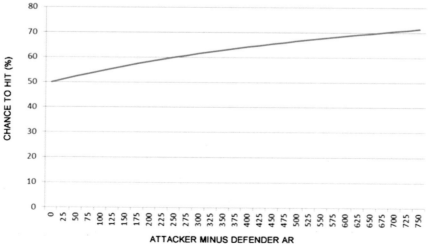

CHANCE TO HIT AN ENEMY OF EQUAL LEVEL AS AR INCREASES

1. The Different Kinds of RPG, and How *Diablo II* Borrows from Them

Investing five stat points (one level's worth) gets a character 25 points of AR, which is the subject of the x-axis. Character level is the other factor under the player's control that affects a character's chances to hit with a physical attack. Below is a graph that shows how gaining levels affects hit chances if attack rating remains static.[10]

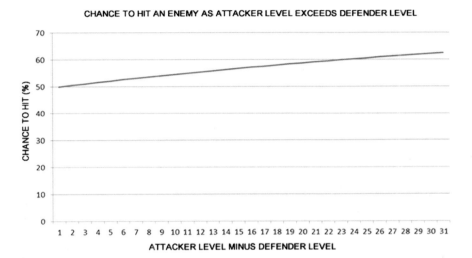

CHANCE TO HIT AN ENEMY AS ATTACKER LEVEL EXCEEDS DEFENDER LEVEL

The slope of the line in the second graph is shallower, although it can be hard to tell just by looking. Even after gaining 30 levels relative to the character's target monster, the chances of hitting only go up by about 12 percentage points. Still, player characters will have a hard time hitting enemies that are a higher level than they are, and an easier time hitting enemies that are a lower level. Although it is never spelled out anywhere in the UI, one of the ways that character classes differ is in the way that level is applied to their hit ratings. Certain classes get bonuses to their "effective level" when making a physical attack. For example, a level 15 Barbarian making a melee attack is treated (for the purposes of hit rating) as though he were actually level 35. That's usually worth about nine percentage points in the chance-to-hit rating (Table 1.1).

Table 1.1 Melee Bonus Levels[11]

Character Class	Bonus Levels When Melee Attacking
Barbarian	+20
Paladin	+20
Assassin	+15
Amazon	+5
Druid	+5
Necromancer	−10
Sorceress	−15

These bonuses mostly make sense. The three characters that tend to fight up close the most often, the Barbarian, Paladin, and Assassin, all get significant bonuses to their effective level. The casters, meanwhile, are penalized when attacking since they really should not be doing so very often. It's the middle two classes, Amazon and Druid, that have problems, but we'll see about those in the respective class situations.

Dexterity, Level, and Block Rate

Dexterity also contributes to defense and blocking, two simulated skills that serve the same ostensible purpose, but which operate independently of one another. Both defense and block rates are responsible for deflecting enemy physical attacks so that they do no damage. Neither has any effect on spells, which are instead governed by elemental resistances. Defense works exactly the same way for the players as it does for the enemies, except that players get to factor dexterity into the equation. The contribution of dexterity isn't much, however.

$$\text{Base Defense Rating} = (\text{Dexterity}/4)^{[12]}$$

Even Amazons and Throw-Barbarians (who put lots of extra points into dexterity) only get the same amount of defense from their dexterity stat that a Paladin gets from a decent helm or boots. All that dexterity isn't really helping the defense stat much. Moreover, defense itself is not that useful. Defense rating only works while the player character is walking or standing (not running), and it's very difficult to get a high enough defense rating for it to help much after level 60. With a skill like the Barbarian's Iron Skin or Paladin's Defiance Aura, defense can be augmented to the point that it offers real protection. Getting a significant amount of defense from items and dexterity alone requires some serious item farming, but we'll cover that in the third section of this book.

The block skill is much more likely to provide significant protection to a player, although it has its drawbacks. Any character that equips a shield (or an Assassin with the Weapon Block skill) can block incoming physical attacks. The primary contributor to the block rating is the shield's own block stat, which is separate from that shield's defense rating.

OCHER TOWER SHIELD OF DEFLECTING
DEFENSE: 22
CHANCE TO BLOCK: 69%
DURABILITY: 60 OF 60
REQUIRED STRENGTH: 76
REQUIRED LEVEL: 9
+30% FASTER BLOCK RATE
20% INCREASED CHANCE OF BLOCKING
LIGHTNING RESIST +20%

The other component in block rating over which the player has control is dexterity. Dexterity improves block rates a lot more than it improves defense, although the required investment is high. Block rate maxes out at 75%.

Below there are two graphs because there are two important dynamics to examine. First, it's a lot easier to reach 75% block by investing in dexterity than it is to reach 75% evasion (armor) rating via defense via any means. In the first graph, the player-character's level is static. The second graph shows what happens to block rate as the player character gains levels.[13,14]

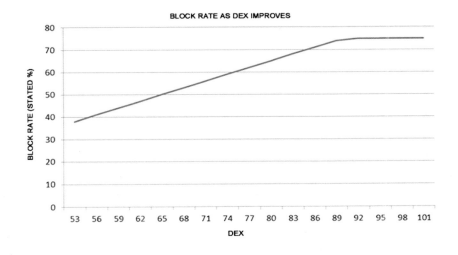

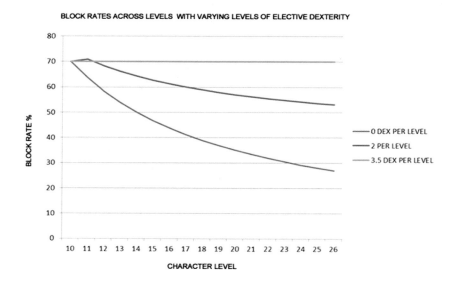

BLOCK RATES ACROSS LEVELS WITH VARYING LEVELS OF ELECTIVE DEXTERITY

Block rates actually go down as the player gains levels unless the player is investing heavily in dexterity. For some dexterity-heavy characters, this isn't a huge problem, but for classes that aren't stacking tons of dexterity, this dynamic forces players to find higher-level shields whose higher block rates can mitigate the lack of dexterity. (Really, all classes benefit from higher-level shields, but the need is greater for classes that don't invest much in dexterity.) Indeed, the class-based differences in shield usage run deeper than dexterity investment. The classes themselves have block rate modifiers that operate similar to the hit rating modifiers. Any given shield has a 10 percentage-point spread for its block rate. For example, if the player equips their character with a Small Shield, the caster classes (Sorceress, Necromancer, and Druid) have a base block rate of 20%, the Paladin has a 30% base block rate, and the Assassin, Amazon, and Barbarian will fall in between at 25%.

Skills

In *Diablo II*, skills themselves have levels that the player can improve. Every time a character gains a level, they gain one skill point that can be invested into any unlocked skill. This is not unique in the history of RPGs; even contemporary games like *World of Warcraft*, *The Witcher*, *Skyrim*, and the *Deus Ex* series use this mechanic. What's unusual about *Diablo II* is the number of times a player can invest in a single skill. Every skill in the game can be leveled up 20 times, although many skills make for very poor investments.

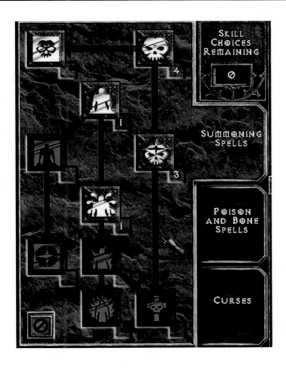

The results of each point are fairly significant as well. Below the next page I have visualized the growth in damage of some of the major skills from a few classes.[15,16]

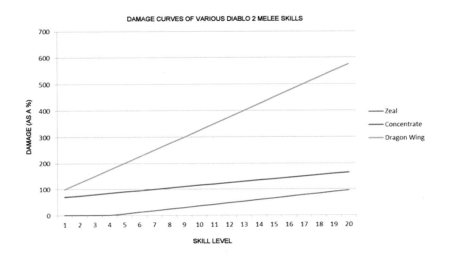

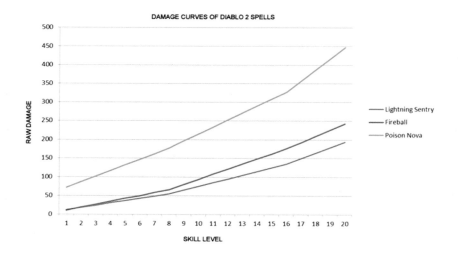

DAMAGE CURVES OF DIABLO 2 SPELLS

(Legend: Lightning Sentry, Fireball, Poison Nova)

The growth is mostly linear, although spells have a little bit of increased slope at the end. The most natural response to this graph is to wonder if the linear growth of monster HP will simply neutralize any gains the player character makes in skill power. The answer is complicated. For the first difficulty setting, and a large part of the second difficulty setting, focused investment in the best skills will give the player increased killing power. In the second half of the game, deficits start to eat away at the player's marginal killing power. At that point, the player has to synthesize gear, skills, and good strategy, but that is the domain of part three of this book.

Elemental Availability

The last major, systemic difference between the character classes is the types of elemental abilities available to each. Including physical-type damage, there are six elemental attributes an attack can have in *Diablo II*. Each class has access to a few elements; none has access to all of them (Table 1.2).

Table 1.2 Elemental Availability Across Character Classes

Class	Fire	Cold	Lightning	Poison	Magic	Physical
Amazon	Yes	Yes	Yes	No	No	No
Assassin	Yes	Yes	Yes	No	No	Yes
Barbarian	No	No	No	No	Yes	Yes
Druid	Yes	Yes	No	Yes	No	Yes
Necromancer	Yes	No	No	Yes	Yes	Yes
Paladin	No	No	Yes	No	Yes	Yes
Sorceress	Yes	Yes	Yes	No	No	No

(Note that this table is made up of *viable* builds. The Assassin has magic damage in the Shadow Arts but doesn't kill with it. The Assassin and Amazon both have poison damage as well, but their poison damage skills are almost universally deprecated, and are not counted.)

You can see how the classes exhibit a great deal of variety in terms of elemental availability, and how there's not a lot of overlap. Six elements are more than enough to make seven classes (and more than a dozen possible builds) distinct in their elemental strengths and weaknesses. Yes, certain classes have a greater ability to split their skill points up between multiple trees than others. The "Meteorb" Sorceress, Tornado/Hurricane Druids, Berserk Barbarians, and Traps Assassins—all of these can mix two elements. Most builds cannot mix three elements without having a very specific gear set, which maintains the game's balance.

In *Diablo II*, the elemental system governs only which creatures or characters take greater or lesser damage from enemy attacks. The balance is mostly orthodox to the RPG tradition, although immunities are occasionally applied in counterintuitive ways. In most RPGs, a creature that is vulnerable to one element is strong against its opposite—icy creatures are vulnerable to fire, and strong against cold, for example. Sometimes that is true in *Diablo II* (certain families of enemy, like the Fallen, share fire resistance), but often elemental strengths and weaknesses don't make any intuitive sense. Thanks to the procedural addition of monster affixes, an enemy can spawn completely immune to fire and ice damage alike. While any unique enemy can spawn with almost any elemental modifier, most of the elemental resistances in the game are fixed. Below are graphs that visualize the prevalence of resistances on the highest difficulty setting—the point at which elemental resistances become common.[17]

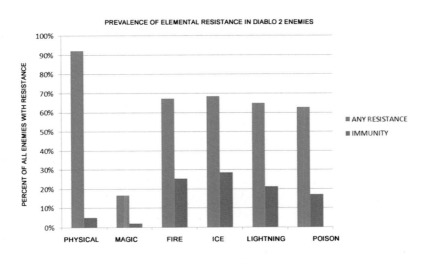

There are a couple of important trends visible here. First, immunities to non-elemental magic and physical damage are much less common than resistances to fire, cold, and lightning. This dynamic is in proportion with the prevalence of extremely powerful fire, cold and lightning attacks in the game, however. These three elements make up 49% of all types of spells or attacks the player can use. But what about resistances that don't reach the level of immunity, and yet are still widespread? The data are clear: physical resistance is extremely common on the highest difficulty setting (although all resistances are higher on that setting). To a certain degree, this makes sense. Physical damage is the most common type of damage; only the Sorceress class lacks a viable build which depends on physical damage. But there seems to be a huge oversight with regards to this dynamic. Physical damage is already subject to another form of mitigation. Skills which deal physical damage are almost always subject to attack rating. This is a disadvantage already; fire magic might be resisted by monsters, but those spells don't miss unless the player aims poorly. Although there are builds that make physical damage viable in late-game *Diablo II*, those builds are a lot harder to make and don't offer much in the way of compensation for that fact. This is a flaw that we'll see come to particular prominence in the bow-using amazon.

Synergies

At high levels, most classes rely on a small number of skills to deal the bulk of their damage. If those skills can only receive 20 skill points worth of investment, what does the player do with surplus skill points? The skill synergy allows one skill to enhance another, allowing players to invest skill points in a way that still enhances their primary skills.

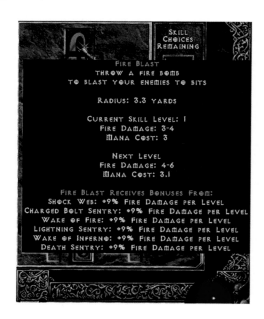

When it comes to synergies, the big difference between classes comes down to the linearity, number degree of their synergies. A linear synergy is any synergy that takes place linearly across a skill tree. For example, the Sorceress's Blizzard skill has synergies from the Frost Bolt, Cold Bolt, and Glacial Spike; those three skills are prerequisites for learning Blizzard, so they are "in line" with the skill. When the player finally does invest in Blizzard, the Sorceress already has a minimum of 15% bonus to its damage. The second important aspect of synergies is their number and degree. Blizzard benefits from three direct synergies, with an average amount of 5% damage per point invested. (I.e., Blizzard has three linear synergies, and their degree is 5% per point.) This means that a player investing all available points into Blizzard synergies might gain as much as a 300% bonus to the damage of the spell. Itemized skill bonuses don't contribute to synergies, but skill damage above level 20 is a little steeper in terms of damage growth, making synergies more valuable. Thus, certain classes have huge advantages in damage because of the linearity and degree of their synergies.

The impact of synergies on character classes is not always strictly quantitative. For example, several of the Barbarian's combat abilities rely on synergies that are non-linear. Both Concentrate and Berserk receive significant amounts of magic damage from skills in the Warcries tree, which is completely independent of the Combat Abilities tree. The Barbarian really does need those Warcries for buffing and crowd control purposes, however. While the Barbarian can't stack points into linear synergies the way that a Sorceress can, his synergies encourage the player to invest in skills with great utility value. This is part of the Barbarian's design philosophy, which requires the use of a movement and crowd control skill in conjunction with a main attack skill. Players tend to build their Sorceresses around one big skill, and then focus on inflating the damage of that skill. For the Barbarian, that strategy doesn't work quite as well, and the synergies reflect it. Similarly, the Necromancer's Curses skill tree lacks synergies entirely. Even the strongest curses won't kill most enemies, so the player needs to pair them with another offensive skill. Although the Poison Nova skill gets synergies from other poison skills, its best complement (what you might call a "soft synergy") comes from the Lower Resist curse, which allows it to do a lot more damage than it normally would. Accordingly, all analysis of a class's synergies will try to take into account what those synergies (or lack of them) mean for the character.

As a last note before diving into the character classes, I want to point out that I have only analyzed the most common builds of each class. I don't delve into the mechanics of unorthodox (but viable) builds like the Double Throw Barbarian, the Whirlwind Assassin or the "Dentist" Necromancer. Even without them, most of the mechanics of each class are represented by the builds I do cover.

Character Classes

Amazon

Builds: 2 – Bowazon (uses bows and the bow/crossbow skill tree) and Javazon (uses javelins and the javelin skill tree)

Bowazon Build

> *Build strength*: Long range, two benefits from dexterity
> *Build weakness*: Low damage, no spells, too many skills to invest in
> *Elemental availability*: Moderate
> *Synergies*: Poor, top-level skills only gain moderate damage from one other
> skill, and there aren't enough skill points to spare to take advantage of it
> *Overview*: The Bowazon is built on classical RPG checks and balances.
> Unfortunately, *Diablo II* is not the kind of game that relies on those things,
> and so the Bowazon ends up a little underpowered relative to her peers.

The great, intrinsic advantages of the Bowazon are her long range and the fact that two benefits are gained from dexterity. As we'll see with several classes, ranged attacks in *Diablo II* are not all equal in effective distance. The Paladin has to be at the center of his target area when casting the Blessed Hammer. The Druid has to be at the center of his Hurricane. Even the Javazon has to be fairly close to reliably hit with her Lightning spells. The Bowazon, like the Traps Assassin and the Sorceress, can sit back at quite a distance, and enjoy the safety that distance affords.

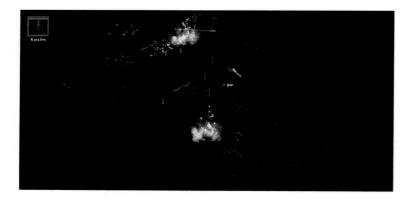

The Bowazon even gets to add the extra protection of having the beefy Valkyrie minion to distract enemies. At high levels, the Valkyrie is hearty enough that it can even tank bosses for a reasonable amount of time, although it has trouble controlling boss aggro. (Technically, the Javazon can also employ a Valkyrie, but the greater range of the Bowazon makes the Valkyrie a little more useful for the latter build.) The Bowazon's other advantage is her ability to gain two benefits from dexterity. As we saw in the section on dexterity, the stat's contribution to hit rating is considerable if the player chooses to stack a lot of it. Because the Bowazon's damage output is also tied to dexterity, she can spend most of her points on it. The problem that we'll end up seeing is that this double advantage simply isn't as strong as it needs to be in order to make up for other weaknesses.

The Bowazon's biggest weakness is that her skills and weapons aren't powerful enough. The big three skills a late-game Bowazon might use, Freezing Arrow, Immolation Arrow, and Strafe simply don't do that much damage.[18]

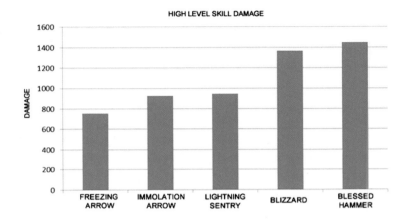

I've visualized the damage of several high-level ranged skills, adding in the main synergies for them. The Bowazon skills come out lower. The other skills visualized are spells. Unlike Bowazon shots, spells never miss (as long as the animation connects with the enemy sprite). To be fair, because the Amazon skills are attacks, they also gain weapon damage not visualized here. But physical resistance is the most common type of resistance, and bows are just not that strong. Below and to the right is a comparison of some bows and melee weapons.[19]

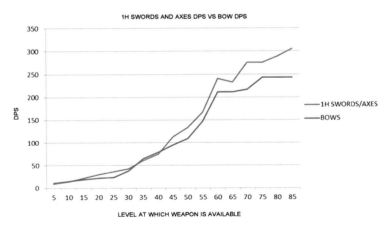

Note that the melee weapons are *one-handed weapons*, and they still surpass bows. That means melee characters are doing more DPS with one hand than Bowazons are with two, meaning they can equip a shield or another weapon. There are definitely bows in the game that make up some of the damage gap, especially through means of very high attack speed, but casters get elite weapons that offer +skill affixes and faster cast rate modifiers, too, so the gap remains.

The real problem is that bows are the victim of traditional balance mechanics that are out of place in a game like *Diablo II*. Ranged weapons face a penalty for the safety they provide by firing at long range. In an orthodox tabletop RPG, they should incur a penalty; that balance is a basic tenet of good design. In the RPGs from which this tenet comes, however, bow-using characters aren't responsible for killing hordes of demons by themselves. In those games, bow-users tend to pick the most dangerous targets and eliminate them tactically while the tanks and melee fighters kill everything else. That's not a viable strategy against the demonic hordes of *Diablo II*. As we've seen, both amazon bows and amazon abilities fall short of their peers. The most elite bows in the game do enough damage to make the Bowazon comparable to other classes, but obtaining them involves killing hordes and hordes of enemies—which is hard to do with her relatively lower power!

There are two places in which the Bowazon might catch up to the other classes: hit rating and in utility/defense skills. All of the Bowazon's damage skills are attacks, and are therefore subject to attack rating (except for Guided Arrow). But, for all their dexterity stacking, amazons don't hit significantly more often than other classes. The biggest reason for this is that neither their weapons nor their skills add that much to attack rating. As we saw in the section on attack rating, the amazon has a lower effective level when striking, losing her about fivepercentage points of hit rating vs the melee classes. Her dexterity provides a nice boost, gaining her back about 14 percentage points. After that, it's all up to weapons and skills.[20]

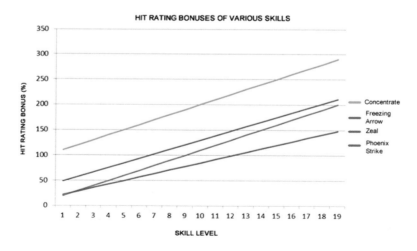

Her skills do not provide her with a significant advantage versus other classes. Moreover, they provide a significantly lower damage multiplier than those other

1. The Different Kinds of RPG, and How *Diablo II* Borrows from Them

skills, especially when we remember that those melee classes are using better weapons. There are still passive skills to consider, however.[21]

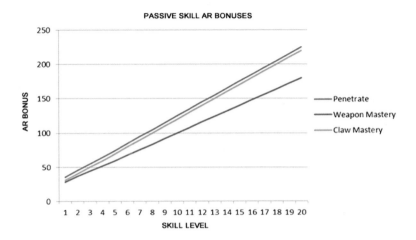

PASSIVE SKILL AR BONUSES

Penetrate keeps up with the other skills, but it doesn't outpace them by an amount that would balance its big flaw. What's not shown here is that Barbarian Weapon Mastery, Paladin Fanaticism, and Assassin Claw Mastery all also provide the character with damage and/or attack speed in addition to hit rating. Penetrate only provides attack rating. Comparatively, the amazon bow passive is just too weak. The designers have simply overcompensated for the Bowazon's range in a way they don't do for Javazons, Traps Assassins, Necromancers, and Elemental Druids.

In theory, all of this could be avoided if the Bowazon's skills gave her more options than other classes have. It seems that this was the designers' intent, but in practice it doesn't compensate for her other shortcomings. The Amazon has an entire skill tree of passive and magic skills that could complement her bow skills reasonably well. Skills like Slow Missiles, Critical Strike, Penetrate, Pierce, Evade, and Dodge would be great if the Bowazon could afford to invest in them heavily. She cannot. Bowazons need to invest 20 points into their main elemental arrow and another 20 into Strafe if they hope to deal any significant damage at all, and then another 20 into Valkyrie. Most players also like to invest in utility skills like Pierce or Guided Arrow. With the prerequisites for those skills, the build barely has any spare points to invest in defensive skills or Critical Strike, and that just isn't enough. Perhaps this is where the Bowazon's class-specific items are supposed to come into play. Even as normal-quality drops, the Amazon-only bows put points into all Bow and Crossbow skills. Is the player supposed to save points in bow skills and reallocate into passive skills? It wouldn't work. The damage and attack rating bonuses in bow skills are too low, so the player must max them out. It appears to be yet another case of over-balancing the Bowazon, forcing her to rely on the elite items that every class wants, but not every class needs. These problems are not fatal; the build is still playable, but for the most part, other builds avoided these kinds of systemic pitfalls.

Javazon Build

> *Build strength*: Medium range, two benefits from core stat, massive splash damage
>
> *Build weakness*: Almost all damage comes from one elemental type
>
> *Elemental availability*: Poor
>
> *Synergies*: The lightning skills are all part of a big linear synergy that makes several of them very powerful
>
> *Overview*: The Javazon has serious limitations, but these limitations are appropriate to the *Diablo II* context. The Javazon is ranged and relatively fragile, but also very powerful. Her big limitation is that almost all of her damage comes from lightning-elemental attacks, meaning that roughly 20% of enemies on hell difficulty are simply immune to the damage she does.

By making one change, the Javazon build corrects the shortcomings of the Bowazon build. Several of the best Javazon skills are spells, and therefore always hit. Thus, the Javazon doesn't have to worry about attack rating as much, nor the extremely widespread resistance to physical damage. The real drawback for the Javazon is that she deals almost all of her damage as lightning, and therefore simply cannot kill enemies who are lightning immune without having rare, resistance-removing gear, or companions who can do that for her. This limitation is one that makes sense for *Diablo II*, however. The Javazon has a strength she can exploit, and a weakness she needs to avoid. The Bowazon is somewhat mediocre across the board. For instance, one solution to the elemental availability problem is to simply avoid lightning immunes; there are plenty of areas in which this is possible. The other solution is to journey with a companion who can lower enemy resistances, like a Necromancer or Paladin. This is exactly the kind of limitation *Diablo II* ought to employ, since the game was explicitly designed to be a multiplayer affair. This doesn't work for the Bowazon, however. There's no location in the game where having underpowered attacks isn't a problem, and there is no party composition that can make a Bowazon more valuable than some other class might be.

It may be the case that the Javazon's greater power is a product of a design problem which the designers knew about but had no solutions for. Like the Sorceress, the Javazon relies on multi-target attacks, especially the tremendous Lightning Fury. Lightning Fury doesn't actually do a ton of damage on its own; most of its strength comes from the number of targets it can hit at one time—more than 20 at higher levels. Lightning Fury also seems to be the "other side of the coin" for Bowazon skills. Although it hits like a spell, Lightning Fury depends on attack speed rather than casting speed. Increased attack speed is an attribute found on items in much greater abundance than faster casting speed. Bowazons benefit from faster attack speed, too, but because that build uses weaker attacks that often miss, this isn't as helpful. For a gigantic explosion of lightning that mows down crowds, increased attack speed is incredibly helpful, and fairly easy to find.

Lightning Fury shares lots of synergy bonuses with several other skills in the lightning tree, making the Javazon build one which is hard to mess up.

You can see how those big synergies allow several skills to be useful against single targets, while Lightning Fury is useful against crowds. The big linear synergy also allows the Javazon's class-specific items to provide considerably more benefit. By adding points to every skill along that linear synergy, the Javazon-specific weapons also trigger all the interlocking synergies. Why couldn't this have been the case for the Bowazon build? Even if the Bowazon fires from longer range, her power isn't reduced proportionally to the advantage that range gives.

Assassin

> *Builds*: 2: Trapsassin, kicksassin

Trapsassin Build

> *Build strength:* Long range, spell damage
> *Build weakness:* Traps can be hard to place in certain tight corridors; fire damage has an effectively shorter range than lightning damage
> *Elemental availability:* Moderate, can deal great fire or lightning damage
> *Synergies:* One of the game's few multi-element linear synergies gives the Trapsassin build some very high damage
> *Overview:* The Trapsassin fires at long range and has two big sources of elemental damage. Her ability to summon a minion also protects her much like the amazon's Valkyrie protects that class. The Trapsassin, however, uses spell damage. Like the Sorceress, she can sit back and let her spells melt enemies she can't even see.

The Assassin who specializes in the Traps skill tree is like the Necromancer or Sorceress, who can easily hit enemies who aren't even on screen. Traps can be placed around corners and they cannot be targeted by the enemy. They can attack independently of the Assassin's primary target, which is a blessing and a curse—sometimes they'll fire on a target other than the one which is the most dangerous. Still, though, their impressive range means that the Trapsassin can usually sit back comfortably while her spells destroy the enemy. This build also has easy access to two elements with enough damage to handle endgame content. This damage depends heavily on the large linear synergies in the traps skill tree.

The synergies for every skill are abundant, but of particular note is the skill Fire Blast, which can gain up to 700% damage increase from its synergies. That skill deals fire damage, and yet it benefits from a huge linear synergy made up of both lightning and fire skills. Thus, the Trapsassin can deal two types of damage in amounts viable for the endgame.

Like staves, wands, and maces, the claw class of weapons frequently comes with +skill modifiers, even on gear that can be purchased from low-level vendors. Unlike those weapons, however, these weapons usually come with category bonuses rather than specific skill bonuses.

Some magical staves, wands, and Necromancer off-hand items have categorical bonuses, but it's a lot more common on claws to see +1 to a skill tree or all

Assassin skills on blue items. The prevalence of categorical bonuses is probably a product of the Assassin's huge, interlocking synergy tree, or the many combos that Kicksassins have to use.

Kicksassin Build

> *Build strength:* Lots of types of damage, finishing moves with a variety of practical effects
>
> *Build weakness:* Not as rugged as Paladin or Barbarian, defensive skills require more micromanagement than in other melee classes
>
> *Elemental availability:* Very high—significant amounts of cold, fire, lightning, or physical damage, plus the attack rating bonuses to actually hit with them
>
> *Synergies:* No big linear synergy chains, but skill synergies mixed with passive skill synergies power the Kicksassin up considerably
>
> *Overview:* The Kicksassin is a melee fighter with a lot of different attacks to use, many of which have elemental components. Her finishing moves have practical effects, and the Shadow Discipline skills give her tons of utility on the battlefield, although it can be difficult to switch to those skills in the heat of battle.

The Assassin who specializes in the martial arts skill tree (typically called a "Kicksassin") can fight in close quarters adeptly, although she uses slightly different means to do so than the Paladin or Barbarian. One of the greatest advantages of the Assassin lies in her elemental availability. The top-level Martial Arts skill, Phoenix Strike, can deal significant amounts of fire, cold, or lightning damage. Given that no enemy in the game can be immune to more than two elements at a time, this means that the Kicksassin will always have an attack that can deal some extra damage.

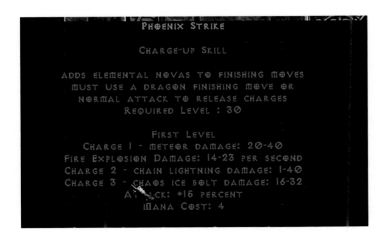

The attack also benefits from some minor synergy bonuses, although the player has to divide skill points between various skills to give each element a synergy boost. The crucial drawback of the attack is that, unlike the skills in the Traps tree, Phoenix Strike is an attack rather than a spell. Thus, in order for Phoenix Strike to hit, the player has to land a physical attack successfully, which may require several attempts at close range. That said, we've already seen in the Bowazon analysis that Assassins get great attack bonuses from Claw Mastery, in addition to gaining damage and critical strike. Moreover, the attack rating bonuses from Phoenix Strike are also great, and combine together to put out damage that is viable for any part of the game. Add to this the practical effects of finishing moves like area damage, teleportation, and major lifesteal and the Assassin can fight just as well as any other melee class.

The Kicksassin's drawback is in its survivability. Although she can equip virtually any armor (as most classes can), her defensive passive abilities aren't enough to allow the Assassin to simply deflect most blows, as a melee Barbarian or shield-using Paladin might do for much of the game. The Assassin's skills help, but she has to rely on some unusual, two-function abilities to do so. Skills like Cloak of Shadows, Burst of Speed, and Fade need to be renewed fairly often, whereas Paladin and Barbarian skills are either inherent or toggled. Burst of Speed and Fade cannot be active at the same time, and so the player has to manage which one is necessary in any individual situation. Similarly, there are spells which help to control crowds, like Psychic Hammer and Mind Blast. The former applies knockback and is useful for keeping approaching crowds away. The latter mind-controls a group of common enemies and makes them fight their allies. Both of these are necessary for good crowd control, but as with the defensive abilities, it can be difficult to switch between them quickly. The *Diablo* UI isn't made for diverse ability usage (this is a topic we'll discuss in the next section) and so the Assassin player has to do more work managing crowds than a Paladin does, for example.

Barbarian

Builds: Not as distinct; Barbarian skill trees don't lock him into skills the way other classes do, except for his chosen Combat Skill. Other than the main Combat Skill, Barbarians can choose from a variety of movement, crowd control, and passive abilities.

Class strength: Very durable, doesn't need to max out many skills to get good use from them

Class weakness: Tends to require use of more skills than other classes do, requires good action mechanics, can run into stalemate situations with enemies who just won't take damage from his physical attacks.

Elemental availability: Poor. He mostly deals physical damage. There are two attacks that deal significant magic damage; one has defensive drawbacks while the other requires major cross-tree synergy investment.

Synergies: The Barbarian's synergies often connect across skill trees, and linear synergies aren't abundant.

Overview: Regardless of which attack skill he wants to use, successful Barbarians need to diversify their skill set a little more than other classes. Barbarians can rely on one skill for killing, but they need movement, crowd control and buffing skills as well

If the primary tactical dilemma of melee fighters in *Diablo II* is the choice between gear that emphasizes attack or survivability, the Barbarian solves that dilemma by allowing the player to complement his choice of gear with abilities that eliminate the drawback. At first glance, this looks like a bit of bad game design. What's the point of creating a tactical decision if the player can just go around it? There are three reasons why the answer to this question is more complicated than traditional game design maxims might lead you to think.

1. To a certain degree, this question is inappropriate for *Diablo II*. There are plenty of gear combinations in *Diablo II* that can turn any character class into a nearly-invincible killing machine. As such, the Barbarian does not violate any of *Diablo II's* major design principles.
2. In another sense, the question is still pertinent, because all of that ludicrously powerful gear is rare and only found at the end of the game. The Barbarian already has some really powerful passive bonuses at level 30. Although the Barbarian doesn't break the game, he can make a dent in the designer's time table.
3. For all his great abilities, the Barbarian never becomes the best at anything. He has the highest possible defense, but that doesn't mean he's the best at avoiding damage. He has great bonuses to hit and attack power and can deal tons of damage, but that doesn't necessarily allow him to chew through enemies as fast as the Sorceress or Hammerdin can. So really, his lack of obvious flaws is checked by a lack of powerful strengths.

In a vacuum, the Barbarian violates many of the traditional RPG tactical balances. In the context of *Diablo II*, the Barbarian makes more sense.

The central tenet of Barbarian design is that he has to use multiple active skills to survive and kill his enemies. All classes invest in multiple skills, of course, but many casters rely on one skill most of the time, while investing the rest in synergies. The Barbarian tends to use several skills more often. This is somewhat like the Assassin, who has to refresh her defensive buffs and control crowds with her Shadow Disciplines skills, but in this case it's primarily an offensive concern. Nearly all Barbarians will use Battle Orders to double their health in the same way that Assassins use Fade. Many of the Barbarian's crowd control skills are also useful killing skills, with way more damage built into them than the Assassin's similar abilities. Barbarians can knock enemies away with Bash on a one-by-one basis, or they can scatter enemies with the AoE (area of effect) Howl ability. Barbarians can even block off parts of the map by using the Grim Totem skill, which lasts for a set amount of time. On the other hand, most Barbarians can only deal significant damage up close, and so he needs to close in on his chosen target—even when something else is in the way. Thus, he has several options for getting closer to enemies. He can use Leap or Leap Attack to jump right on an enemy. He can use the Taunt ability to draw enemies to himself, especially in conjunction with Howl.

He can also use the passive skills Increased Stamina and Increased Speed to simply run to his targets faster than other enemies can intercept him. We're going to cover this in a lot more depth in the section on action mechanics, but what should be clear is that the Barbarian has a variety of ways to get around the battlefield—especially when moving towards an enemy.

The Barbarian also has several different ways to do his killing. Regardless of the minutiae of builds, there are two primary choices that the designers set up for Barbarian players. The first decision is whether players want to sacrifice defense to deal damage or not. The second choice is whether players want to use fast weapons or powerful ones. The choices are not binary; players can sacrifice some defense or all of it, and can choose weapons on a spectrum of speeds and powers.

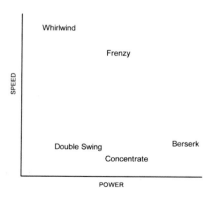

There are a lot of subsequent decisions to make here. Magic damage, the Barbarian's one alternative to physical damage, exists on both ends of the spectrum. With a synergy from Battle Orders, Concentrate can gain magic damage equal to its physical damage while still providing significant bonuses to defense. Berserk, on the other end of the spectrum, provides a lot more magical damage, but it sets the Barbarian's defense rating to zero while active. Moreover, Berserk removes all effects like lifesteal (which does exactly what it sounds like) and so removes the best auxiliary defense mechanism a Barbarian might have. Frenzy and Whirlwind, the other two melee attacks that are viable at high level, are in the middle. Frenzy does not directly impair defense, but it does require the Barbarian to set down his shield. Whirlwind also does not affect defense, but the Barbarian cannot use potions while in the middle of it, nor redirect his path.

The other dimension along which Barbarian attacks can be measured is their need for attack speed, as increased by items. This is one part of this document that theorycrafters (ultra-hardcore players who use advanced mathematics to create perfect characters) will object to. Most serious *Diablo II* players insist on maximum attack speed in their melee builds, no matter how hard it is to obtain it. I agree that, if you were trying to build the perfect killing machine, you should have the maximum possible attack speed all the time. To accomplish this, most serious players will also perform thousands of repetitive runs, lasting literally hundreds of hours. The game was not designed to force all players into this behavior. Attack speed, as implemented by the *Diablo II* designers, has a diminishing returns curve built in.[22]

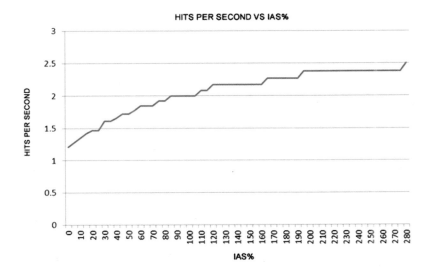

These diminishing returns are in place to force the average player (who is not willing to do hundreds of hours of Lower Kurast runs, for example) to build around what he or she lacks. Because of the diminishing returns on attack speed, players who already have fairly high attack speed aren't going to get as much return on more items or skills which add to it. The reverse is also true. If a Barbarian has high damage, but little attack speed, his player will have an easier time acquiring a little bit of attack speed through his skills than acquiring marginally higher damage on his weapon. The Whirlwind skill breaks this dynamic a little bit, in that its gains from attack speed are greater than those of other skills. Whirlwind has its own hit-check table that is a little more favorable to attack speed, although it, too, suffers from diminishing returns. The last consideration for Whirlwind is that it costs the same amount of mana no matter how many hits it outputs, so higher attack speed gives the player more hits per mana, even at short distances—explaining its position on the diagram.

To summarize the essence of the Barbarian, I want to point to a set of his most important passive skills: Masteries. Skills like Sword Mastery and Polearm Mastery show how building a Barbarian is a much more reactive process than building other classes. There isn't just one such mastery skill; each weapon type has its own skill. Although character construction is all about tactical choices, the split in weapon mastery skills seems unnecessarily punitive. If the player commits to one type of weapon, do they have to throw away all the other weapon types they get on their journey through the game? This way of thinking gets the Barbarian build exactly backwards. The point of weapon masteries is not to proscribe weapon types, but to adapt to what the player encounters. By saving some skill points, the player can wait for a great weapon to drop and then invest in the appropriate mastery. This is what the Barbarian is like, generally. The Barbarian can choose what passives skills, movement skills, and attacking skills best complement the gear he actually has. For most other classes, players choose a build and then seek out the best items for it. Master-level players do the same for Barbarian, but for most players, the Barbarian allows for a little more flexibility and reactive play.

Necromancer

Builds: 2: Bone/Poison and Summoner

Bone/Poison Necro

Build Strength: Ranged character with terrific crowd control abilities and great itemized skill bonuses.

Build Weakness: Direct damage build has to work a little harder for damage than his fellow casters.

Elemental Availability: Good, can reliably inflict poison and non-elemental magic. Skilled players can inflict fire damage, although it requires certain battlefield conditions. Can mitigate enemy resistances, in any case.

Synergies: No huge, linear synergies in the manner of the Sorceress, Trapsassin, or Hammerdin, but all curses are synergistic with other spells, by design.

Overview: A more technically advanced caster, the bone/poison Necromancer is nevertheless a powerful class when played by an experienced player. Instead of dealing tons of damage directly, the Necromancer uses curses to weaken his opponents before hitting them with sources of damage. Minor skills in the Poison & Bone tree also work as great crowd control effects with minimal investment. The Necromancer's peculiar itemization also works to enhance his power in orthogonal ways.

The most important thing to know about the Necromancer's spells is that they simply lack the top-end damage of the Sorceress, Hammerdin, Trapsassin, or Hurricane Druid. Factor in the Lower Resist curse, and suddenly the build makes a lot more sense for poison damage builds. (Lower Resist does not affect pure magic resistance for some reason, although the bone spells are still useful as supplemental damage.) The Necromancer also has other advantages over his fellow casters, mostly in the form of utility skills. Regardless of character class, the average player is going to build their character around three primary skills, investing 20 points into each, plus about 5–10 points into all the prerequisites that unlock those skills. Most players aren't going to use those prerequisites in high-level play, because they're too weak. The Necromancer is one class where that weakness is not a problem. Curses like Decrepify are still reasonably useful at low levels, and Bone Wall can easily be spammed to clutter the map and prevent enemies from advancing too quickly. The poison Necromancer will still probably focus on three spells (like Poison Nova, Bone Spirit, and Lower Resist), but he's got other options as well.

Necromancer itemization is a little unusual as well. The Necromancer's class-specific item is normal in that it has class-specific +skill affixes. It's unusual in that it occupies the shield slot, meaning that the Necromancer can also equip a wand which has even more +skill bonuses. In the earlier parts of the game, this makes it easy for casual Necromancers to build up skills above their character's level. At the highest levels, the powerful unique items available to all casters neutralize this advantage. Another quirk of Necromancer itemization is the unusual prevalence of faster cast rate (FCR) affixes on Necromancer items. The FCR affix is equally useful for all casters, but Necromancers have a much easier time accumulating a significant amount on relatively common gear. Thus, the relatively low damage of a spell like Bone Spirit can be augmented by a much faster cast rate.

Summoner

Build Strength: Offloads the responsibility for fighting (and tanking) enemies on to the Necromancer's minions, allowing the Necromancer to throw curses and spells from the back.

Build Weakness: Depends on the availability of enemy corpses. Consumes more skill points than the poison/bone build, reducing the Necromancer's utility. Summons sometimes have trouble standing up to boss monsters.

Elemental Availability: Poor. The Summoner relies on his minions' physical damage, and in some cases, moderate fire damage from a golem. The Necromancer can mitigate this with curses, however.

Synergies: The Summoning tree has numerous passive bonuses which grant increased health, power, and even resistance to summoned monsters, but these bonuses are more complicated than similar bonuses in other classes and builds. Curses operate synergistically with any build.

Overview: The Summoner build requires lots of management, but greatly reduces the danger to the Necromancer by putting an army of minions between him and the enemy. At higher levels, these minions can easily handle enemy swarms, but they have trouble with bosses unless the player manages the Necromancer minions very carefully. The biggest problem is that the player is not limited by mana, but rather by the supply of enemy corpses.

The Summoner Necromancer is able to raise an army of skeletons or resurrected enemies, as well as one golem. The most important design dynamic for the Summoner is that the strength of skeletons and golems is dependent only on the Necromancer's skill levels, whereas the strength of enemies raised by the Revive skill depends also on the strength of the enemy raised. The two sets of skills share some passive abilities (Skeleton Mastery and Summon Resist), but otherwise present a problem for players. How should Necromancer skill points be invested? A Sorceress's early investments into low-level skills are usually synergistic with her top-level skills. Investments into Raise Skeleton do not help the late-game Necromancer in the same way, but the Summoner needs those points in Raise Skeleton in order to survive the early game. Patch 1.13 allows players to reallocate all their talent points later in the game, but for more than a decade, this wasn't possible. This didn't make the Necromancer unplayable; he is and has been a fun and powerful character. This lack of early-skill-to-late-skill synergy is unusual among *Diablo II* characters, however, and it's curious that the designers never addressed it in any of the numerous patches that came before 1.13.

Summoner mechanics are also unique, although there is much of difference between the use of skeletons, golems, and revived monsters. The easy part of the Summoner build is that the player can simply sit back and cast a few curses while his minions do most of the work. The hard part is keeping all those minions alive, especially against bosses. Skeletons, golems, and revived monsters are always dying, and the Necromancer has to replace them by reanimating another corpse. Most of the time, this is not a problem, since *Diablo II* sends the player through thousands of monsters. Bosses, however, present a problem. Unique enemies, with their enhanced power, can easily kill all of the player's minions without yielding any new corpses to raise. This sends the player running around the map, trying to raise a new army while a unique monster chases them. The effect is even worse with the act bosses, who (with the exception of *Diablo*) all wait in a relatively small location with few enemies to raise. Expert players eventually figure out that certain revived monsters are better for bosses than others, but no other class has to go and track down a certain pack of enemies every time they want to farm the act bosses.

The problem of facing bosses as a Summoner or "minion master" (as the class is more generally called) is one that is repeated in many different games. Both the original *Guild Wars* and *Hellgate: London* (another Brevik game) put their minion masters through similar difficulties when taking on bosses. Minions in those games are more than adequate for common trash mobs, but are often inadequate for dealing or surviving damage from bosses. Although he didn't address this topic specifically, David Brevik commented to me that he thought there were certain unsolvable problems in RPG design—like perfectly balancing AoE spell damage.[23] If many different game companies cannot balance the minion master even with the advantage of lots of hindsight, then we shouldn't fault the designers of *Diablo II* for a relatively small imperfection. After all, the Summoner build is still viable, even if players face an uneven challenge when playing it.

Paladin

> *Builds*: 3: Fanatidin, Smiter, Hammerdin (the former two are both melee)

Fanatidin/Smiter

> *Build Strengths*: High defense and damage output, can get attack speed from a skill instead of an item, can wear a shield and block at a high rate.
> *Build Weaknesses*: Somewhat limited elemental availability in his highest-damage skills.
> *Elemental availability*: Theoretically high, as he has abundant physical and magical damage, and can add several other elements to his physical attack via Vengeance. That said, Paladins rarely choose this last option as it is mutually exclusive with better attacks. So the effective elemental availability is much lower than it seems.
> *Synergies*: Unremarkable, medium-strength synergies.
> *Overview*: The Smiter and Fanatidin are different in one key dynamic: the former is better against single targets and the latter against multiple. They are both melee fighters, however, and primarily deal physical damage.

The Paladin class is naturally durable, thanks to good bonuses from vitality and the highest natural block rate in the game. Indeed, even a low-level use of Holy Shield can max out the block rate of an otherwise mediocre shield. These two melee classes are viable for just that reason. Many newer players prefer the Fanatidin because of Fanaticism's numerous, large bonuses. Indeed, Fanaticism is one of the few skills in the game that gives significant attack speed bonuses without compromising defense (as Frenzy incidentally does), or locking out other skills (as shapeshifting skills do). Its bonuses to damage and attack rating also scale well and can make even simple builds with low-level gear into effective killing machines. More experienced players often prefer the Smiter build for its high top-end damage against single targets. These players tend to run (or teleport) right for bosses. Both builds rely on a similar setup and similar gear, however, and are mechanically very easy. By and large, the player clicks on a target until it dies. All of the effort in building one of these Paladins is in preparation and gear.

Hammerdin

> *Build Strengths*: Huge ranged damage, can still wear great armor and have a high block rate.
> *Build Weaknesses*: Very limited elemental availability.
> *Elemental Availability*: Very poor, only does magic damage.
> *Synergies*: Benefits from one of the most infamous skill synergies in the game
> *Overview*: The Paladin is also a competent caster class and can use magical combat skills to destroy his opponents at range. One would expect, based on the setup of his physical skills, that the Paladin's magical options would be divided between single-target and multi-target spells, but it isn't so.

Both the Blessed Hammer and Fist of the Heavens spells are meant to hit multiple targets, and they both do a good job of it. The problem is that Blessed Hammer enjoys one of the only multiplicative synergies in the game. As we saw in the amazon section, the Paladin's bonuses to hit rating and damage are comparable to any class's best passive skills. Blessed Aim, Might, and Fanaticism, are a great help to a melee Paladin and his melee friends. None of them can match what concentration does for Blessed Hammer, though. Blessed Hammer's normal synergy is from Sacrifice/Blessed Aim. It gains 12% more damage per level of either; 20 levels in either will multiply the power of Blessed Hammer by 2.4. Normally, the synergy from Concentration would simply add to the multiplier. A 240% bonus from Concentration would normally be added to the 240% bonus from Sacrifice to provide a 480% bonus. Instead, Concentration does this:

$$(\text{Blessed hammer} * 2.4) * 2.4 \ [=5.76]$$

In later levels when the player has lots of +skill affixes on their gear, the returns on this equation erupt in tremendous fashion. Almost all of the power of the Hammerdin comes down to this one equation and its deviation from the normal mechanics of *Diablo II*. (It also explains why the Hammerdin is ludicrously popular to people who know about the math.)

Druid

> *Builds*: 3: Elemental, Shapeshifter, Summoner (though this last build isn't really used)

Elemental Druid

> *Build Strengths*: Powerful ranged caster, wide variety of elemental options in one talent tree.
> *Build Weaknesses*: Without significant use of synergies, spells do less damage than other casters.

Elemental Availability: High, can use spells that deal cold, fire, and physical damage.

Synergies: There are abundant and powerful linear synergies, but these only bring the spells up to the level of other casters. In essence, the Druid has to spend more skill points than the Sorceress to achieve the same damage.

Overview: The Druid is a great example of traditional balance ideas implemented in the context of *Diablo II*. Although the elemental Druid can mix and match different elemental skills fairly easily, his abilities don't naturally put out as much damage as less flexible classes like the Sorceress or Hammerdin.

The Elemental Druid is one of the few builds that has three or more types of elemental damage available in one skill tree, and the only one that has that damage available as entirely spells rather than as attacks.

Accordingly, the Druid can mix and match elements quite easily, thus avoiding the trap of elemental resistance on the hardest difficulty. The Druid sacrifices damage to do this; most of his skills are only half to three-quarters as strong as their analogues in the Sorceress skill trees. Moreover, the Druid has no powerful passive or aura as the Sorceress and Paladin do. What the Elemental Druid does have is a set of powerful linear synergies. Particularly in the fire elemental sub-tree, the player can raise the damage of spells like Armageddon to levels roughly comparable with other casting classes. By spending that many points in synergies, though, the Druid loses utility. This is exactly the kind of balance dynamic one would expect from an orthodox RPG. *Diablo II* isn't that kind of RPG, however. The point of the game is to become an unstoppable killing machine, so this balance dynamic seems a little out of place. It doesn't ruin the game; other classes can choose versatility over concentrated power as well. The Druid just has a much easier and more obvious choice.

The place where the Elemental Druid really gets hurt by the extra skill points needed for top-end damage is in his ability to dabble in summoning skills. There is no truly viable Summoner build for Druids, but the summoned minions can be useful for soaking up damage or providing utility skills. A Druid trying to put 80 skill points into elemental spells and synergies doesn't really have room to take advantage of that. Although extraneous or unusable character builds are a fixture of otherwise great titles in RPG history, *Diablo II* doesn't really contain any totally useless skill trees. The summoning tree isn't useless, but it's not always easy for Elemental Druids to take advantage of it.

Shapeshifter (Bear/Wolf) Druid

Build Strengths: Although this is a melee build, it has access to several significant sources of elemental damage as well. This build also has relatively fine control over its balance of tankiness or deadliness.

Build Weaknesses: Although this build has a variety of passive abilities and attacks, Druids who change into the bear or wolf form can only use one spell.

Elemental Availability: High for a melee class; they can output significant physical and fire damage and have a passable poison option.

Synergies: Synergies provide elemental options, but require large investments for viable effects.

Overview: The shapeshifter build transforms the Druid into a strong melee fighter at the cost of his utility. Wolf and bear Druids are every bit the fighting equals of other melee classes but are a little more confined in terms of action abilities than their peers.

The Shapeshifter Druid transforms into a wolf or bear, gaining large bonuses to attack rating, moderate damage increases, and a variety of specific skills. One of the curious things about the shapeshifting skills tree is that although many of its skills are actually active skills that require continual refreshing, they operate like passive skills. Werebear and Werewolf, for example, only provide passive bonuses to stats, but they cannot be toggled. Rabies and Feral Rage both operate like passive skills as well, but must be cast. Fire Claws, Shock Wave, and Fury operate more like the combat skills of other classes, but all of them are enhanced versions of the basic attack. Sometimes the Shapeshifter Druid can feel a little monotonous for this reason, until he reaches higher levels and can diversify his skills a little bit. Nevertheless, Shapeshifter Druids can be powerful. Fury, for example, is a more powerful version of the Paladin's Zeal skill, with the various passive and pseudo-passive skills standing in for fanaticism. One problem the Shapeshifter Druid has is that he cannot cast most of the spells in the Elemental Skill tree. The only spell he can cast is Armageddon, which is a decent source of fire damage, but it requires lots of investment in synergies to become really powerful, and eats up mana that this build doesn't always have. Most of his best attacks are physical, naturally, but he has another source of fire damage and a somewhat useful poison damage skill. Fire Claws is naturally weak (topping out around 400 damage per strike at level 20) and seems, at first glance, like it would only be useful during the mid-game. Fire Claws also has one of the largest synergies in the game. It's not a linear synergy; all of the contributing skills are actually in the Elemental Skills tree. There are five synergetic skills, and all of them offer a 22% bonus to Fire Claws per level, giving the Shapeshifter Druid the power to deal thousands of fire damage if he commits to the synergy. Unlike Armageddon, this skill doesn't consume much mana, and relies on attack speed rather than casting speed. It's a big commitment in terms of skill points, but is a viable means of delivering elemental damage.

The Druid also has a similar ability to deal significant poison damage by means of a large synergy. The Rabies skill has a neat perk: the poison spreads from enemy to enemy. Thus, in large crowds, the player can infect quite a few targets with a decent amount of poison damage. The problem is that it's poison damage, which is generally difficult to use in *Diablo II*. *Diablo II* is so fast-paced that poison damage, which takes place over several seconds, doesn't always kill fast enough. Rabies damage scales nicely, but the time component also scales up.[24]

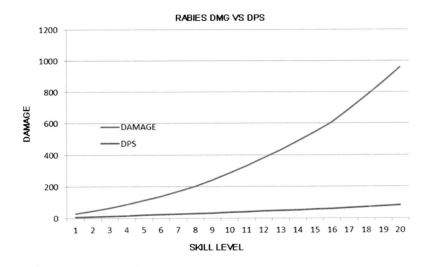

The player can get around this with mob-tagging behaviors and lots of +skill affix items, but great gear will make any build work. Rabies is a cool skill, but it has a systemic handicap in that almost all poison skills (except for Poison Nova) are hurt by expanding time denominators.

Sorceress

> *Builds*: 3: Fire, Cold, and Lightning. Technically, there are sub-builds of these three elements, but the mechanical differences and strategy are not different between those builds in the same way that the Hammerdin is different from the Fanatidin.
>
> *Class Strengths*: Can easily put out tons of ranged damage, uses spells exclusively, has the best mobility skill in the game.
>
> *Class Weaknesses*: Most fragile character in the game.
>
> *Elemental availability*: High, can use Fire, Cold or Lightning. Can use any two of those if the player is willing to trade away some top-end damage.
>
> *Synergies*: Has large, linear synergies for the highest-damage skills in every tree, plus strong, synergistic passive skills.
>
> *Overview*: A relatively straightforward class with some obvious drawbacks, the Sorceress is easy to build and play through the first two difficulty settings but faces the same late-game problems as every other class.

From a mechanics standpoint, the Sorceress is probably the simplest class in the game. The player chooses a target and fires spells at it until it dies. There's not much else for the Sorceress to do except run (or teleport) away from approaching enemies. The Cold Sorceress is the only version with significant crowd control abilities, and she trades damage (as all cold abilities do) for this effect. The overall strategy of the Cold Sorceress doesn't differ that much from the Fire or Lightning Sorceresses; the player still keeps enemies at a distance. Likewise, Cold Sorceresses can use spells to increase their armor, and Lightning Sorceresses can increase their effective health (through Energy Shield), but the player should still be fighting at range. There are other small differences between the types of Sorceresses. Lightning and Fire Sorceresses benefit a little more from faster cast rate affixes than Cold Sorceresses do, but all the classes benefit most from +skill affixes and mana. Moreover, no affix or skill radically changes the way that the Sorceress class is played.

Although I'll address it again later, I want to mention Teleport, the Sorceress's mobility skill. The interesting thing about teleport, from the perspective of character classes, is that it embodies the Sorceress's design philosophy so well. Teleport is a terrific mobility skill, but unlike the similar skills of other classes, it doesn't have a landing effect. Thus, Teleport is much better at getting the Sorceress out of battle than into it. This is exactly what we would expect from a class that is always supposed to be firing from range and avoiding contact at all costs.

The Action RPG and *Diablo II's* Action Heritage

Diablo, the predecessor to *Diablo II*, began its life as a fairly orthodox roguelike. While the project was still early in development, the main Blizzard team that oversaw the project told David Brevik that the game engine should work in real time. This decision changed the course of development in a big way, and introduced many important game design ideas that are not native to the roguelike subgenre. Because it started as a roguelike, *Diablo's* relationship to its roguelike source material is fairly straightforward; it adapts roguelike concepts for a mass-market audience. The relationship between *Diablo II* and its action-game ancestors is more complicated and theoretical. One of *Diablo II's* greatest achievements is the way it recreates the fundamental structure of action games (Nishikado motion) through procedural means. This section will look at the action heritage of *Diablo II* and explain the way it reinterprets that heritage through an RPG lens.

One issue I want to tackle before looking at the history of the action RPG is how to define the level-up. Critics and fans have argued about the point at which an action game has enough RPG content that it becomes a true action RPG, instead of just being an action or action-adventure game. (David Brevik himself pondered this question in another interview[25] without coming to a conclusive answer.) For example, many question whether *The Legend of Zelda* games are really RPGs. I say that they are, because Link can gain more health, magic, strength, etc. over time. These gains are usually not connected to experience points, nor are they part of explicit "character levels," but does that mean the game is not an RPG? For me, *Zelda* is still an RPG, because these things are still level-ups. A level-up is a permanent, periodic increase in the power of a player-character. When Link gains more heart containers, his maximum life is permanently increased, and that permanency makes it a level-up. When he gains the use of the Master Sword, it represents a significant increase in power over the starting sword, and he has it for the rest of the game. These gains are all connected to finding loot, but as we'll see many more times in this book, loot is often the most important kind of level-up. Link makes one or more of these gains in every major dungeon. The period is simply measured in dungeons rather than being measured in EXP. Whether or not you agree, this definition is enormously important to the rest of this book.

The Birth of the Action RPG

Once RPGs started to appear on PC and home videogame consoles, it was inevitable that design ideas would leak between the booming world of digital action games and the older world of tabletop RPGs. For designers of RPGs, this was a boon, for it gave them another way to escape from the overshadowing influence of *D&D*. For all of its systemic completeness, *D&D* never implemented the kind of real-time dexterity challenges found in action games like *Space Invaders*, *Pac-Man*, or *Galaga*. (It's difficult to imagine exactly how it could do so, to be fair.) By implementing action-game challenges against a background of RPG systems, designers could combine their favorite parts of RPGs with any of the various action subgenres. The result would be a hybrid game that felt significantly different from either of its parents. I call this the *combination* strategy, which allows designers to disguise relatively old RPG tropes in the clothes of an action game.

The action RPG had a major and immediate historical impact on the design—and audience—of RPGs. For one thing, the action RPG was the genre that introduced the RPG form to console gamers who had never seen it on the tabletop. Games like *The Legend of Zelda, Gauntlet, Golden Axe, Secret of Mana,* and *Ys* taught console game players how to play RPGs by allowing them to rely on their existing action-game skills to compensate for their lack of RPG knowledge.

Two Difficulty Curves

The first game that is still relevant to the history of action game design is *Space Invaders* (1978). The designer of that game, Tomohiro Nishikado, was also the engineer responsible for the construction of its arcade machinery. Because of the technical limitations of the processor he used, Nishikado discovered that the aliens moved faster when there were fewer of them on screen.

 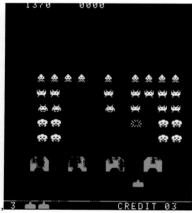

This causes each level in the game to become more difficult as the player progresses through it. Rather than correct for this unusual property, Nishikado kept it as a design feature. Indeed, he embellished it by making each successive level start at a slightly higher level of difficulty, thus reiterating his serendipitous difficulty structure at the macro level.

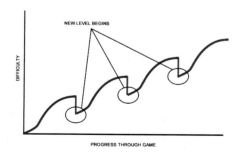

1. The Different Kinds of RPG, and How *Diablo II* Borrows from Them

I call this up-and-down motion in videogame difficulty *Nishikado motion*. Nishikado motion is the fundamental structure that underpins nearly all of mainstream videogame design. Even today in the era of extensive player psychology research and interest-curve diagrams, Nishikado motion remains the central pillar of mainstream videogame design.

Difficulty in traditional RPGs is structured very differently than it is in mainstream videogames. Games of all kinds teach the skills that players need to learn in order to overcome later challenges. In action games, players can often fail to learn, might only partially learn, or might even forget the dexterity skills that a game teaches. Players of action games can also become literally exhausted by the demands of a fast-paced action game, and their hand-eye coordination can suffer after levels as short as a few minutes. Nishikado motion accommodates this by routinely delivering lulls in the intense action, to let the player regain their stamina and catch up on skills they lack, or that they have forgotten. Traditional RPGs are different. In an RPG, the player's character does most of the learning. It's the character who learns how to pick locks, cast fireballs, parry sword-strikes, and speak with animals. The player just has to declare the action and roll dice. Thus, RPGs can afford a more linear difficulty curve. What's more, because most things in a traditional RPG depend on statistics, it's actually a lot easier for RPG designers to precisely tune their difficulty curves. This is not to say that all RPGs are perfectly linear in terms of difficulty. Even the best RPGs are inconsistent from quest to quest if the player hasn't made certain choices, but the overall emphasis on undulating arcs of difficulty is less prevalent (and less necessary) in tabletop-style RPGs than it is in console videogames.

Although traditional RPGs are probably a little easier to balance than action games of equal scope, certain RPGs are harder to balance than others. *Diablo II*, like most games that have some roguelike DNA, has an occasional balance issue stemming from its widespread use of randomness and procedural generation. *Diablo II's* volatility is a little different from its roguelike counterparts in that there's a much greater emphasis on positive variation. That is, in *Rogue*, *Angband* and *Moria*, lucky players will barely finish the hardest challenges. In *Diablo II*, lucky players can quickly become unstoppable demigods. This is an intentional design decision, one that shaped that everything in *Diablo II*, from the construction of monsters to the way that loot tables work. One of the most interesting things we'll see about *Diablo II's* difficulty, however, is that it is very similar to the up-and-down rhythm of Nishikado motion. It's not exactly the same, but it's clearly analogous. I call this type of difficulty curve *Schaefer variation*, after the Schafer brothers, one of whom (Max) first explained the phenomenon to me, and who continue to use the structure in the *Torchlight* series. (I want to note here that Brevik and designer Stieg Hedlund also had a considerable role in shaping this design structure; it was clearly a group effort. Moreover, Brevik has toyed with the dynamic in his later games as well.)[26,27] Schaefer variation is simply Nishikado motion accomplished through procedural means. In Chapter 3 of this book, we'll take a look at the exact details of how this happens, but the idea of Schaefer variation is an important one throughout this book.

The Action Parts of *Diablo II*

The influence of the action genre runs much deeper in *Diablo II* than merely theoretical ideas. *Diablo II* is definitely an action game, and its action mechanics shape the player's experience in ways that separate it from other games in the same genre. No two action RPGs are the same in the way that they balance and mix their action and RPG components. For example, the most famous action RPG series of all time, *The Legend of Zelda*, depends heavily upon the non-combat applications of its action mechanics. Whether it's hitting switches with a boomerang, leaping chasms with a hookshot, or lighting a series of torches before the first one burns out, there are many tasks that depend on player dexterity and sense of timing but do not involve combat. During those moments, the game almost moves entirely into the action genre. Thus, we could say that *Zelda* games depend a lot more on their action components than *Diablo II* does. *Diablo's* action mechanics are almost entirely built around combat. In the moments when they're not fighting, by contrast, players of *Diablo II* are doing things like crafting or managing gear, which is a part of the game that depends almost entirely on RPG systems. The only action mechanic that the player uses outside of combat is enhanced movement for exploring dungeons, like Teleport, Leap, or Burst of Speed. Then again, all exploration in *Diablo II* is frequently interrupted by combat. When we talk about the role of the action genre in *Diablo II*, we're talking about combat.

Diablo was originally conceived as a traditional, turn-based roguelike. When the game was altered to operate in real time, many of its fundamental RPG mechanics had to change as well. Traditional RPGs take place in discrete turns. Each player-character or enemy gets a chance to act in the order that their simulated skills and chance allow. During their turns, each character can move once and attack once, with some small variations. What happens to this time-tested procedure when real time is applied, and everyone is taking their "turn" at once? All those mechanics either need to be adapted or dropped. For the most part, *Diablo II* adapts them to real time in straightforward, intuitive ways that place most of the emphasis on simulated skills, but there are some action-specific adaptations as well. The following section will analyze each of the ways that *Diablo II* adapts RPG ideas into an action context, and the implications for the game as a whole. Some of this material was briefly covered in the character class section, but here we'll spend more time on the exact mechanical operation of action abilities with an emphasis on quantitative analysis and diagramming.

Movement

Most movement in *Diablo II* is uncomplicated. All characters move at a speed measured in yards per second. Characters run 50% faster than they walk, but while running, they have no effective defense rating. There are lots of items that grant increased movement speed, especially unique boots and magical charms.

Many expert players seek to max out their movement speed through these items as an essential part of farming/leveling runs. Like many of the things that these players seek to max out, these bonuses suffer significant diminishing returns as the character nears maximum speed.

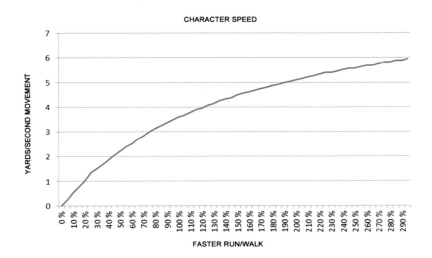

The gains in speed flatten out quickly. Diminishing returns on real-time effects is a theme we'll be revisiting often in this section. While many ultra-hardcore players still insist on having maximum speed, these diminishing returns are in place to encourage players to seek a more balanced approach to their gear. That said, speed bonuses granted by abilities (like Vigor or Burst of Speed) do not experience diminishing returns when combined with other speed bonuses—although the skills do grant lower bonuses per point invested in them. I will discuss movement abilities in their own section, below.

Monster Movement

Monsters in *Diablo II* mostly follow the same rules as players. They have set run and walk speeds, although these can be increased by affixes and auras. Some monsters can leap and teleport, much like player characters can, although they appear to wait much longer between uses of these abilities than players do— probably because of a special timer built into their movement behavior, or else every battle would be nearly as difficult as player-vs-player combat. There are several monster affixes that enhance their speed as well. Champions and Fanatic enemies move faster than normal, and any unique enemy with the "extra fast" affix will move at double speed. Because these speed bonuses are based on abilities rather than gear (which enemies don't wear), the enemy speed bonus does not experience diminishing returns, and so some of the fastest enemies in the game can become terrifyingly fast if they happen to fall within a movement speed buff of a procedurally spawned enemy. This is one of the ways in which we'll see (in Chapter 3) how the difficulty of the game can suddenly spike thanks to unfortunate procedural generation.

There are two modes of enemy movement that the player doesn't have: flying and phasing. The Scavenger class of enemies can fly over the battlefield, immune to all attacks, before landing to strike (below, left).

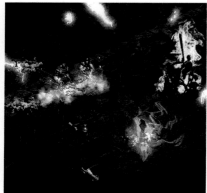

This is the only family of enemies which moves like this, and it gives the enemy minimal advantage, as they cannot attack while in flight. Similarly, *Black Souls* (above, right) can phase out of reality, becoming hard to see (and therefore hit) while moving. The Black Soul can be exceedingly dangerous because of how quickly it can phase in, take a shot at the player, and then phase out again. Although many movement abilities (like the Cave Leaper's jump) are annoying to deal with, this is the only one that makes an enemy significantly more dangerous without a procedurally added affix.

Player Characters and Their Movement Options

With one (glaring) exception, melee classes have the best special movement options. Like basic movement, these abilities are not especially complicated. The rules are as follows:

1. The player-character must have line of sight to the target location
2. The ending location of the ability must be navigable (not a wall or a pit)
3. There must be no impassable obstructions between the character and the ending destination

These rules are fairly straightforward. The first two apply to all movement skills equally; the last rule varies in its application from skill to skill. Ground-based movement abilities are subject to enemy attacks and can be stopped as such; a leaping Barbarian does not have the same problem. Ease of movement isn't the only factor in the utility of a movement skill, however. Other things like movement speed, movement distance, mana and time costs, and impact on enemies all affect the usefulness of an ability. The Paladin and Barbarian movement skills have reasonably strong attacks built into them but aren't terribly fast or far-reaching. The Assassin's Burst of Speed ability is easy to sustain indefinitely and includes an attack buff but is easily stopped. The Sorceress's Teleport is twice as expensive as other movement skills, and has no effect on enemies, and it leaves the caster somewhat vulnerable. Yet, Teleport can move the player across the landscape faster than any other skill in the game, and doesn't collide with terrain objects except map edges. Many of the game's most popular items (like the coveted Enigma runeword) offer the Teleport skill to non-Sorceresses as their primary benefit. The skill is simply too desirable to pass up.

There are three great object lessons about game design that we can learn from the way that movement abilities in *Diablo II* are configured. The first lesson is that, if you're designing an action RPG, you can bet that players will find ways to employ action solutions to your RPG problems. One theme common to action games of all genres (whether platformers, survival horror or anything in the open-world format) is that players eventually learn to avoid most enemies. Many enemies offer either no reward, or only a trivial one. In a game with powerful running and jumping abilities, it is easy (and sensible) for the player to avoid all of these encounters. (There is an entire genre of YouTube videos where players do this for long stretches in *Dark/Demon's Souls* games.) Sure enough, that's what experienced players in *Diablo II* do. Whether it's rushing to Baal or Mephisto, or running around Lower Kurast looking for the infamous super-chests located there, players use their character's movement skills to exploit all manner of shortcut and AI patterns in order not to fight enemies. This is yet another area in which the Teleport skill is overpowered; it deals no damage and has no stun or knockback effects. It doesn't need them, though, if the player is simply avoiding combat.

That last point makes for a good segue into the second lesson, which is that qualitative differences are not the same as tactical balances. Both of those things are necessary parts of a good class system. In the previous three *Reverse Designs*, I made the case that qualitative differences in videogame design are greatly underappreciated. I maintain that stance here, with one important caveat: qualitative differences only matter if the quantitative differences don't make them obsolete. If there are two paths through a game, and one of them is much harder than the other without any commensurate reward, it doesn't matter if they're qualitatively different. Players are going to choose based on difficulty. The same thing applies to RPG abilities. It doesn't matter how great the Barbarian and Paladin movement skills feel—though they do make you feel like a badass when you use them right—if they lag way behind Teleport in speed and range. It's tempting to counter this with "but Sorceresses are fragile!" That's correct, but remember that we're talking about mobility and avoiding enemies here. Fragility hardly matters if the player is deftly zooming past anything dangerous. In order for players to be able to choose freely among qualitatively different options, those options must be roughly equal in effectiveness.

The third lesson we can learn from movement skills in *Diablo II* is that there are always lots of creative solutions to game design problems, but those solutions need to make sense in the context of the game they apply to. The problem with movement in *Diablo II* is that Teleport is too powerful, and the designers knew it. Teleport is also far too resonant with the Sorceress class—and really, the game in general—for the designers to remove or nerf it too harshly. Their solution was to offer Teleport to any class on a variety of items like amulets, staves, or even armor. This is the quintessential *Diablo II* strategy. The design philosophy of *Diablo II* includes the tenet that any character should be able to become an overpowered demigod. Teleportation is a part of that strategy, and inasmuch as any class can gain Teleport, it makes sense in the context of *Diablo II*. Rather than nerf one class and its abilities, the designers simply make the other classes more powerful by addition.

Crowd Control Skills

Only a few classes have skills that greatly enhance their movement. All classes, however, have the reverse, skills that make enemies slower or stop them entirely. We've already covered some of this in the section on character classes, but here we're going to pay more attention to the particular action dynamics of the various crowd control abilities in the game. One of the most common problems in *Diablo II*, especially for inexperienced players, is becoming surrounded by enemies.

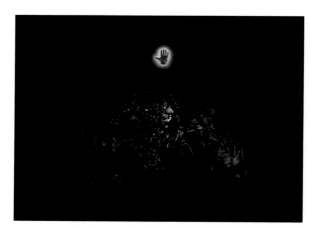

In large numbers, these enemies can even kill player-characters whom they ordinarily could hardly touch. What can a player do if they lack the escape skills like Teleport or Leap—or can't use them because the crowd of enemies is too big?

The answer is, of course, crowd control skills, which either restrict or redirect the movement of that enemy mob.

The first thing to understand when it comes to crowd control dynamics in *Diablo II* is how the enemy AI controls those crowds. Brevik and Hedlund both explained that, except for bosses, AI in the game is very rudimentary.[29,30] Most normal enemies can idle, move, or attack. Some enemies also have a simple evasion script, like the Dark Archer, who will flee the player to perform a ranged attack, or the Cave Leaper, who only comes into melee range to make brief hit-and-run strikes. Aside from these occasional, small variations, common enemies operate in the traditional videogame herd. A herd is any group of enemies whose primary movement pattern is to simply collapse on the player. In the diagram below, the red circles are enemies, and the blue one is the player.

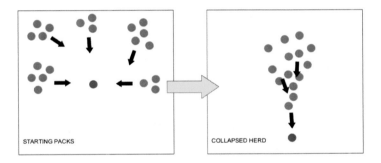

No matter what shape a herd begins in, the enemies in that herd will collapse to form an amorphous blob around their target. The player can take advantage of this in a few ways, with or without crowd control abilities. With a few exceptions (Ghosts, flying enemies), enemies cannot move through one another. Because their AI is so rudimentary, large groups of enemies of roughly similar speed will slowly get stretched out in a path moving toward the player. The herd and its three basic shapes (initial placement, amorphous blob, and stretched-out) are an important to the way that crowd control works, as we'll see below.

Categories of Crowd Control Skills

There are three categories of crowd control skills: slows, repels, and distractions. All of these are useful, but they have different effects on the real-time crowds that the game hurls at the player over and over. Slows reduce the movement of enemies in a group. (Note that I include all stuns in the slow category because the crowd-control impact of stuns is essentially the same as those of slow effects.) The most prevalent example of the slow-type debuff is the chill effect from cold damage.

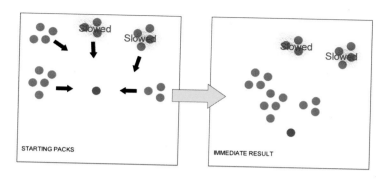

STARTING PACKS — IMMEDIATE RESULT

Most cold damage slows an enemy by about half, although this can vary based on the source and the target in question. Because all cold attacks apply this debuff, cold damage is weaker than other elemental damage of the same level. For example, the level-35 affix for cold damage on magical weapons adds an average of 25 cold damage to an attack, while the fire-based suffix of the same level, adds 56 damage.[31] There are also a few cold attacks, like Frost Nova, which trades away 75% of its damage (compared to same-level spells) for three times the freeze duration. This is merely an extension of the same principle that underlies all cold damage. Similarly, some cold attacks can freeze enemies solid. Like all stuns, this is just a more extreme slow, but it also trades away even more damage to achieve the highest level of crowd control.

Slow effects can also be administered through a Necromancer curse, or through a weapon affix, which appears on unique and set items. Obviously, only the Necromancer can use curses, but the slow applied by items is also limited. As with most slows, the classes that benefit from the weapon-based slows are ranged. By slowing a herd of enemies, the player gains separation from them, and can subsequently pummel them from a distance. It's a little strange that of the unique weapons which have a slow effect, 10 are melee weapons and only two are ranged. (Ranged weapons have yet another small drawback.) Nevertheless, curses and weapon-based slows stack additively with cold and with each other, and can greatly reduce enemy movement speed. There is a cap to the amount of slowing that an enemy can receive (an 85% reduction in speed or one yard per second, whichever is higher), although nothing in the game indicates this.

Regardless of the type or degree of slow inflicted, there are specific action-oriented effects of using this type of crowd control. In the context of small groups of enemies, slowing effects are simple and have predictable impacts on the herd.

Slow effects delay the threat from one or more of these converging herds. In the small groups that populate many narrower areas, this works great, but not all crowds of enemies are so small or move in toward the player piecemeal. Some herds number in the dozens and come in an indistinct blob. These groups have different dynamics when it comes to slow effects. With a few exceptions (ghosts, teleporting enemies, flying creatures), monsters cannot move through one another. Thus, enemies under the effects of a slowing debuff become a natural barrier, while giving a new shape to a large collapsing herd.

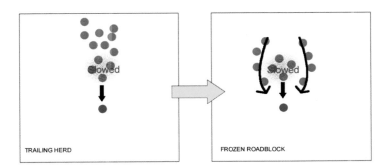

Shooting a cold ability or other slow into a crowd can actually cause secondary problems if the radius of the slowing effect is not large. The enemies will split up to come around their slowed comrades, and in doing so, spread out. For a ranged caster who's kiting a herd (leading a herd while firing at a distance), this creates more diffuse targets, requiring more spells or more kiting. This is not a huge problem, but it's one that could be solved by the right shape of attack. The "Cone of Cold" is an attack dating back into the tabletop years, and cone-shaped attacks are plentiful in the action game heritage. The lack of such an attack in *Diablo II* is a little strange. *Diablo II* does use a few cone-shaped and linear attacks, but none of them are cold-elemental. It's not a game-breaking deficiency by any means, but it is a curious omission.

Repelling Attacks

The second type of crowd control attack is the repelling type, which does not (usually) slow or stop enemies, but forces them to move away from the source of the attack. There are four characteristics that define a repelling skill: shape, source, distance, and duration. Some repelling skills, mostly those connected to melee combat, are radial in shape.

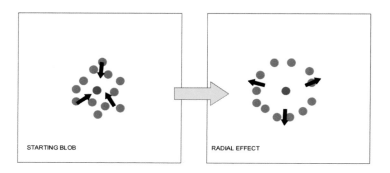

The Barbarian's Howl skill is the best example of this, but certain weapons and armor (the unique helm Howltusk, for example) also repel enemies within a small radius of the character who equips them. Weapons only cause one monster to flee at a time, but the AoE abilities that use this kind of repelling attack don't allow players to be selective in which enemies they target. All nearby enemies will run away. This seems like it would hurt melee attackers who need to get in close to at least one enemy, but this problem is somewhat mitigated by the fact that radial repelling skills don't have a huge area of effect, nor a long period of effect. Duration and distance are an important part of repelling skills. The small window of time and space afforded by radial skills like Howl give the player just enough time to target the most dangerous enemy of the group with an engage skill like Leap Attack. This is useful for sorting through crowds more than it is for getting out of them entirely.

The other major shape for repelling crowd control abilities is the linear shape. This type of crowd control includes most knockback skills, which target either one or a small group of enemies which are knocked away from the attacking character in a straight line. Because of the low number of targets on most of these skills, this type doesn't control "crowds" quite as much as it controls individual members of that crowd. Knockback skills tend to be cheap and high-damage relative to other crowd control skills. Knockback is also usually the property of an attack rather than a spell. So, on the one hand, it can miss its target. On the other hand, it is one of the few types of crowd control that can easily be combined with other types. Even low-level gear and abilities can grant a clever player the means to both knock back and chill his or her enemies. Indeed, this is a good way to increase the effective duration and distance of knockback. Those two dimensions are an important part of all crowd control skills, but knockback offers little separation and very little duration. Thus, those combinatoric possibilities are key to the knockback's long-term utility.

Outsourcing the Slow and Repel

Slow and repel attacks have different dynamics if the source of the skill is not the player-character's body. The clearest example of this is Necromancer curses, which can inflict a variety of crowd-controlling debuffs, like slow. This spell is in the typical radial shape, but it's centered on the player's mouse click, rather than on the character's body. This affords the player a lot more discretion in changing the shape of a collapsing herd, and also allows players to use the ability without having to wait until enemies are on top of their characters. Similarly, the Barbarian can use a radial repel attack, Grim Ward, which can be placed on the battlefield. Although its radius isn't very large, the ability to place it away from the Barbarian gives the player an advantageous angle on enemy movements, and the totem can even obstruct passageways in dungeon settings. The Necromancer's Bone Wall is similar in effect, but linear in shape.

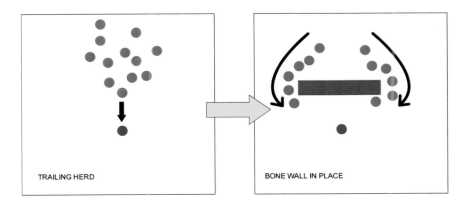

Knockback is perpendicular to the player, while the linear shape of Bone Wall runs, when placed, parallel to the player. Although Bone Wall blocks more than it repels, it nevertheless has largely the same bottleneck-creating effect as Grim Ward when used in the right spot. Putting it in the right spot is fairly easy, though, because the source isn't the player.

Enemy Infighting

Certain abilities can cause enemies to target members of their own group with attacks. The notable examples of this type of crowd control are the Assassin skill

---

Mind Blast and the Necromancer curse Attract. If you don't consider monster stats, these crowd control abilities are balanced sensibly. Both Attract and Mind Blast have small effect radii compared to other debuffs. Attract does not work on boss mobs; Mind Blast only has a low chance of controlling enemy monsters. When used, they still distract enemies from attacking the player, and they still create the wedge around which unaffected monsters have to walk, although the size of the effect is noticeably smaller. All of this seems like a fair tradeoff if the debuff is going to cause monsters to deal damage to one another, taking some of the burden off the player.

The problem with the balance of enemy infighting abilities is that enemies deal very little damage compared to the amount of HP they have. In fact, you can barely see the HP if you put it on a graph with damage.[32]

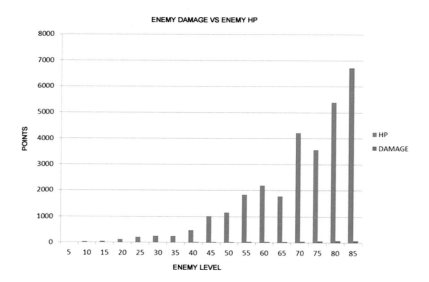

This dynamic exists because *Diablo II* puts much more emphasis on killing power than it does on character survivability. The most HP a player character could reasonably accumulate is around six thousand (without having to sacrifice every other stat). A damage-focused character with the same amount of time invested might be able to output four or five times that much damage per second. Thus, enemies have tons of HP on the harder difficulty settings, but deal relatively little damage. Any skill that causes a monster to damage itself or another monster just isn't going to be significant. These skills do a reasonable job of keeping enemies occupied, but Mind Blast doesn't last very long, and Attract is overwritten by any curse which might actually help the Necromancer deal damage to those targets. Other crowd control skills are simply more useful.

Key Lessons from Crowd Control

Crowd control skills in *Diablo II* teach a clear and widely applicable lesson about action skills in an RPG. Although all the crowd controls are meant to be different—meant for different characters and contexts—certain characteristics that they share can make them more or less powerful. For example, the shape of a crowd control skill doesn't matter very much. As long as a linear crowd control can affect more than one enemy (as Bone Wall does), and the player can aim it well, it can be as effective as a radial crowd control (like Psychic Hammer). On the other hand, the source of a crowd control skill affects its utility immensely. Howl is a useful skill that sends enemies running away from the Barbarian, but Grim Ward and Terror can do the same thing at essentially any point on the screen, offering the player the same effect with more versatility. Finally, longer durations are a huge asset to crowd control, but are also the first target of balancing efforts. The most common crowd control effect, chill from cold spells, is also the one to which all enemies gain resistance on higher difficulties. The chill effect in hell difficulty lasts for only a fraction of the length it does on normal. Less common sources of crowd control effects don't suffer from diminished effect on higher difficulties, which is a pretty typical balance dynamic for an RPG. Rarer skills and items tend to be better than common ones.

The UI Problem

For all the nuance and complexity built into the action abilities in *Diablo II*, using those abilities is occasionally difficult because of the antiquated UI. I want to say up front that in its own time, *Diablo II* offered a slick player experience. The part of the UI which matters the most, targeting enemies with skills, works quite well. Right-clicking to target with a spell is natural and has the precision of mouse movement. Moreover, hitboxes in *Diablo II* are on the generous side for most monsters.

That said, sometimes certain terrain doodads also have these larger hitboxes and can block shots you wouldn't expect. Moreover, in large crowds, it's hard to target a single enemy because of the overlapping hitboxes. Some of this is probably intentional; it should be hard to hit enemies in large crowds. In any case, it's not the kind of game where it matters which enemy the player hits first—at least not often.

The real problem with *Diablo II's* UI is how difficult it is to switch between skills. We just saw two whole sections about the many action applications of movement and crowd control abilities. It's not unusual at all for a good player to switch between a movement ability, a primary attack and a crowd control skill, or even two of each, but how should the player switch between them? The big limiting factor is that the player's primary hand cannot leave the mouse. For people who don't have a deluxe gaming mouse, that leaves five fingers on the other hand that the player can use. Four of those fingers are dedicated to potions most of the time. The thumb can handle the item drops or the "hold still" command (with some button remapping). The designers found themselves without a convenient solution for switching between a variety of skills. They went with the obvious (but somewhat inconvenient) solution of using scroll wheels or the function keys.

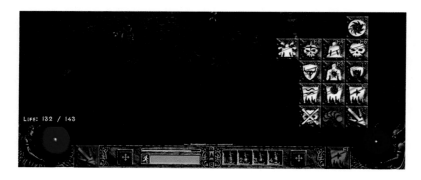

The lower part of the QWERTY keyboard is standardized, so the designers can design and playtest for it without having to do extra research. Everything above the standard QWERTY layout and letters can vary significantly across different models and eras. The space between the number row and the function keys (which can be assigned to abilities) can vary between different models of keyboards. The alignment of the function keys can vary. The size and texture of the function keys can vary. The average human hand can't comfortably reach more than two function keys without having to move the entire arm a little bit. The muscle movements of the arm (especially the non-dominant arm) are not nearly as precise for most people as those of the hand, and can cost precious milliseconds while the player is in combat. What's more, the player cannot look away from the screen because the game is so fast-paced.

There are quite a few problems with the configuration of *Diablo II's* keyboard controls, but none of them are actually fatal to the game. With some practice, players can either reprogram their keyboard or learn to use the first few function keys reasonably well. The player can also use the scroll wheel on the mouse to cycle through abilities, but that isn't as precise as analogous controls in other action games. Because *Diablo II's* systems are so fun to use, players will adapt, but they shouldn't have to. One of the few things that *Diablo III* unequivocally improved over its ancestor was the design of the hotbar. In that game, the player has easy access to six abilities and a potion by only moving their fingers. I'm ambivalent about the change in potion consumption rates (and health systems in general) in *Diablo III*, but some kind of change had to happen in order to facilitate easier ability use.

I realize that it's somewhat unfair to criticize *Diablo II* for not inventing keyboard setups that didn't exist at the time. The design of action keyboard maps and quick UIs were largely driven by the FPS boom of the early 2000s. Millions of dollars of playtesting went into the creation of those games, and each one learned from the errors of the games that came before it. I still point out the problem, however, because it's important to the history of action RPG design. Perhaps the exact changes which *Diablo III* used to allow players to mix abilities weren't perfect, but it should be clear that they were necessary, and why.

Looking Back at Action Mechanics in *Diablo II*

Although *Diablo* began its life as a turn-based roguelike, by the time of *Diablo II* the designers had put a lot of thought into the implications of including action mechanics in their game. Special abilities for crowd control and character movement show that the design team didn't just import traditional role playing ideas into the action space without thoughtful adaptation. Not only do the movement abilities of each class feel different, but they also match the design philosophies of the characters that use them. Whether it's chilling enemies, stunning them, knocking them back, scaring them away, putting up walls, or even causing enemies to fight amongst themselves, there are many ways for the characters to deal with dangerous swarms. None of these abilities are merely token efforts, either. If used correctly, each class's abilities are useful and distinct from what the other classes have. This brings up another important aspect of the influence of the action genre on *Diablo II*. When a game mixes genres well (what I have elsewhere called a composite game), it is possible for the player to use the mechanics of one genre to solve the problems of the other. Good action mechanics in *Diablo II* can absolutely make up for statistical shortfalls, especially in the early game. Good use of kiting and crowd control can allow fledgling casters to over-perform their early damage and mana shortages. Movement skills, meanwhile, can help melee classes target the most dangerous members of enemy packs and eliminate the unique and champion enemies who present a real threat, early in the game. Whereas a good command of the action mechanics is nice to have early, it becomes essential in the late game. Bad action mechanics can cost even well-built characters some deaths if the player strays carelessly into situations no character can reasonably survive. Action mechanics could easily have been a place where the designers simply added real time without any depth, but they took the time and care to make sure that the action part of the *Diablo* formula shines through.

The Different Kinds of Randomness in *Diablo II*

Students enter game design programs with many prejudices about game design that need to be amended. One of the most common prejudices I have encountered among students is the notion that all randomness in game design is more or less the same. This idea springs from a lack of critical examination. Often, I've asked students about these small fireballs that periodically fly through the screen in *Super Mario World*.

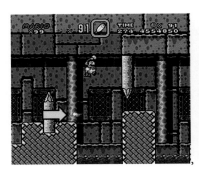 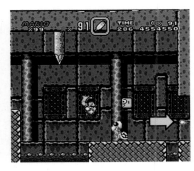

Students tend to say that these fireballs come at random. I then ask, "So they can come at any time or not come at all?" All students quickly figure out that this isn't the case. Even brief observation reveals that the fireballs come at a regular rate. I then ask more questions about fireball speed, fireball quantity, etc. Eventually, the students figure out that certain things are true of the fireball and the randomness to which it is subject. The truth is that only fireball position is variable. The quantity, frequency, speed and size of the fireballs are not random at all. Indeed, even their position is restricted to about half the screen. With a little bit of critical examination, young designers learn that randomness in game design is actually much more nuanced than a cursory glance might tell them. This statement is especially true of *Diablo II*. Not only is the use of randomness nuanced and complex, there are also many different kinds of randomness built into the systems that make up the game. This chapter of the book examines the different kinds of randomness built into the systems of *Diablo II*.

Intro to Types of Randomness

Diablo II makes for a great lesson in the various kinds of randomness that exist in game design because it employs so many of them. Indeed, not only does *Diablo II* exhibit many kinds of randomness, but it also causes many of these random systems to interact with one another in complex ways. By studying *Diablo II*, we can learn a lot, generally, about randomness in game design. The first step in this study, naturally, is to identify all of the kinds of randomness that exist in the game and explain how they work. One proviso I want to offer before I begin, however, is that I am only going to offer game-specific definitions of the various kinds of randomness. I am certain that there are mathematics-specific or science-specific definitions of the things I am about to describe. I don't know them and I don't need to because I'm not really trying to define widely-applicable statistical concepts. For the purposes of this book, I'm only interested in creating some simple frameworks for understanding randomness in game design. Many readers who have statistical training might object to my characterizations of randomness as being too simple. Moreover, many of the things I describe are just different ways of looking at the same basic concept. All of those objections are totally true! But many of the descriptions that follow are still useful for thinking about videogame design, and hopefully do not distort or dissemble about the deeper concepts they represent.

Randomness within a Range

The most obvious and most traditional type of randomness in *Diablo II* is what I call randomness within a range, or "RR" for short. Randomness within a range is what most people have in mind when they think about randomness. For example, if you ask someone to think of a random number, they'll probably think of an integer between one and ten, or maybe one and 100. That's an assumption English speakers tend to share. A truly random number could be anything from seven to pi squared to 41,286,317.91—or literally anything else! Like most people, however, *Diablo* uses randomness within a certain range to control the number of possibilities.

2. The Different Kinds of Randomness in *Diablo II*

Diablo II uses RR copiously: the damage done by almost every attack made by a player character or enemy exists in RR format in more than one way. This has a profound effect on the way that *Diablo II* operates because of the difference between how people perceive randomness and how the game displays it. For an RPG, *Diablo II* is very fast and very intense, and players and enemies can easily use thousands of attacks per hour. Thus, the player's perception of the power of an attack depends on the average damage of that attack (or set of attacks). When adopting a new attack or weapon, players will notice if the average damage is significantly higher very quickly as they chew through hundreds of enemies at a faster rate. Large increases (or decreases) in damage are not the problem—the problem lies in marginal increases and the way that the game's UI displays RR-format damage.

The character screen displays damage in RR format rather than in average format. It's not hard to calculate the average of two numbers, but *Diablo II* isn't the kind of game where players are meant to keep a scratchpad or calculator handy. Some RPGs are like that. In 5th Edition *D&D*, each round of combat takes six in-game seconds, but probably takes 90 seconds to five minutes to actually play out in real time, depending on how many players there are. There's plenty of time during those rounds to do a little math and sort out which weapon or skill to use. If *Diablo II* were played that way, players would never make it out of the first dungeon—there are just too many enemies to fight and too many weapons and attacks to choose from.

How big of a problem does the lack of an average figure present to players who aren't slowing down the game to do the basic math when presented with alternatives? Let's say a *Diablo II* player is presented with two magic swords to pick from. The swords have the exact same base stats, 16–28 damage (22 damage average), but they have different magical modifiers. The first sword has a magical modifier that gives it +10 to maximum damage. The second sword has a magical modifier that gives it +10 to minimum damage. Which one is better? Over a long enough sample, neither one is better, although minimum damage increases are significantly rarer as affixes. The only tactical advantage for higher minimum damage is when hunting a very specific sort of monster. If the player knows the average HP of an enemy he or she is hunting, and can get the minimum damage of the character's weapon or attack above it, minimum damage is a little more valuable. Overkilling enemies doesn't help. That said, there's no long-term reason why there should be separate benefits to maximum and minimum damage at all. Weapon affixes that augment minimum and maximum damage aren't a huge part of the game; most of the high-end equipment offers a percentage-based increase. The principle is still important, because when players select between different skill-based attacks, they get information (and decisions to make based on it) that is just not that useful to them most of the time.

RR Randomness and Encounter Dynamics

The slightly murky nature of randomness within a range is not without its merits, however, even when it's at its murkiest. Monster HP also exists within a random range of values, and this range creates some interesting action effects. The Fallen has an average of 209 HP on nightmare difficulty,[33] but it can have anywhere from 131 to 288 HP as well. Because each member of a pack can have different HP, these random variations can have some interesting results when a player uses a multi-target attack. Below I have visualized a group of Fallen before and after a multi-target attack like Glacial Spike.

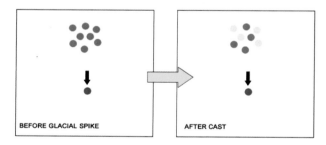

What's happened here is that, as the sorceress casts her spells, the monsters begin to close in on her. Some of the monsters with lower HP die, but their HP is random, meaning that the remaining pack of higher-HP monsters takes on an irregular shape. This shape then gives the player a tactical new choice of where to run in order to launch the next few spells. This is one of the better examples of how randomness in RPG systems can lead to action-game consequences. The player isn't aware of this (because the random damage and random enemy HP are not displayed numerically), but it nevertheless succeeds at forcing the player to make tactical choices in real time.

But this One Goes Up to 11

True to roguelike orthodoxy, but often quite frustrating to mainstream audiences, *Diablo II*'s best weapons and armor all exhibit RR variation in the affixes they

2. The Different Kinds of Randomness in *Diablo II*

acquire. The best one-handed sword in the game (Azurewrath), for example, can have an increased damage affix of anywhere from 230% to 270%. This can give fits to master-level players who spend hundreds of hours trying to find *any* version of the item, but who all want the perfect version. Anyone doing the math on the variation will notice, however, that the RR variation can only change Azurewrath's DPS by about 30 damage, or less than two percent. Not all items are like this. Another sword called The Grandfather, for example, experiences a 100 percentage-point RR variation, and accordingly it can see its DPS change by about 23% based on the stats it drops with.[34] The damage modifiers on most weapons vary less than 50 percentage points, however, and even that level is uncommon except on elite, unique two-handed weapons.

The bigger problem is in the smaller ranges. Items like the unique helm Valkyrie Wing offer affixes like +1–2 to amazon skills. At the highest levels, it's easy for the player to make up for the loss of 30 DPS, but +skill affixes are as valuable at level five as they are at level 85. (Some top-end melee builds do not need such affixes at all, but most classes benefit from them greatly.) Ondal's Wisdom, a late game staff, is always one of the most valuable caster weapons in the game. It offers 45% faster cast rate, 40–50 energy, and 5% bonus experience; it's a tremendous item, but it also offers +2–4 to all skills.[35] The high end of that range is worth a lot more than the low end, and players will rightly be frustrated if they get a two rather than a three or a four. We'll see in Chapter 3 of this book how those affixes change the overall value of an item, but it suffices to say for now that small RR variation in very important stats is far more important than large-range variation in DPS. This doesn't mean that players will throw away unique items that don't have perfect stats. Unique items are rare enough that players can't throw high-level items away crassly. Unique items also tend to be powerful in several different ways, and some of those ways are bound to be useful to the player. We'll see a lot more about this aspect of unique items in Chapter 3.

RR and Map Generation

Although its implementation is not nearly as obvious as elsewhere, *Diablo II* also employs RR variation in map construction. The procedural generation of maps is one place where the otherwise thorough documentation of *Diablo II* falls short. (This is probably because the most advanced players of *Diablo II* employ map-hacks, which reveal the entire map and thereby obviate the need for a comprehensive understanding of map generation.) Moreover, the *Diablo* creators I interviewed were not able to recall every step of their methods perfectly. They did provide me with quite a bit of info on the general process, however. This process will come up again in the "deck of cards" randomness section, but I mention it here because there is a bit of RR variation in it, too. The overall process is as follows:

1. The overall size of the map is determined
2. The orientation of the map is determined
3. The zone created is wrapped in a containing wall, which has its own generation algorithm

4. The major feature of the zone is placed
5. Rooms and/or doodad objects like trees or houses are added to fill the space (deck of cards randomness, which we'll examine later)
6. Enemies are added based on density limits (also deck of cards randomness)[36-38]

It's not immediately clear how some of these steps are governed by RR, but they are. Map size, for example, is always calculated within a pre-set range. The X and Y axes of a map have minimums and maximums, and the total area of each zone also has a cap. The specifics of each zone aren't terribly relevant, but some zones are meant to be bigger than others. Acts one and two have large, rectangular outdoor zones punctuated by dungeons that are narrow and more corridor-like. Act three, by contrast, has long, snaking outdoor zones which tend to follow the path of an impossibly meandering river. There's not a predetermined length, but rather an RR guideline that determines the map length.

In the fourth step of the map generation process, the algorithm places a zone's main feature. Usually this feature is the entrance to a dungeon, like the Cairn Stones in Stony Field, or a portal into a demonic realm in the Act five maps. Sometimes the object is simply a quest objective too, like the Tree of Inifus in the Dark Wood. Regardless, the designers made some guidelines to prevent key map objects from colliding with other objects that would prevent access.

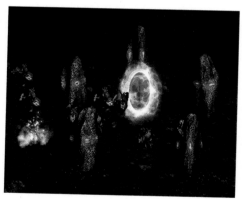

In most cases, this object cannot be placed next to the edge of the zone. To accomplish this, the designers employed a range that looks something like this:

Object Location

XCoordinate = (X-Axis + 20 yards) to (X-AxisMaximum − 20 yards)

YCoordinate = (Y-Axis + 20 yards) to (Y-AxisMaximum − 20 yards)

(Nobody had the exact formulas, but this example reflects the philosophy which the designers did remember.) Thus, the most important object in the zone is

2. The Different Kinds of Randomness in *Diablo II*

algorithmically separated from being next to a large barrier object which might block or glitch it.

Key Lessons from Randomness within a Range

- The most important thing to know about RR variation is that players will perceive the average of your range, even if they don't know what that average is. Just tell players what the average is
- Small ranges (1–2) are more volatile than large ranges (1–100) when you're dealing with important stats like DPS or skill modifiers—but large ranges on items can leave some players bitter over significant reductions in power
- RR variation is a great way to set bounds on objects in the map without setting a fixed location

Slice-of-Pie Randomness

Slice-of-pie (SOP) randomness is the kind of randomness that occurs when there are several random options, any of which could be the outcome of a given roll. Rather than give an example from everyday life, I'm going to dive right into the *Diablo*-specific applications of it. This type of randomness governs most of the steps in loot generation, including the first step. When an enemy dies, the game looks at that monster's level and then pulls from a list of items of that level or lower. This means that the monster could drop a level 35 item, a level six item, or nothing at all—but not with equal probability.[39]

CHANCE OF ITEM DROP BY iLEVEL

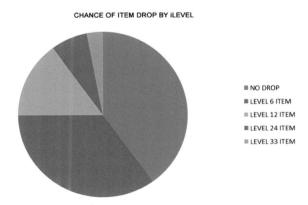

- NO DROP
- LEVEL 6 ITEM
- LEVEL 12 ITEM
- LEVEL 24 ITEM
- LEVEL 33 ITEM

Each slice of the pie is a different size. Why use a pie-shaped visualization, though? There are three properties of this kind of randomness that are best understood when the entire process is viewed as selecting one piece of a pie. The first property is that, when the game selects a piece of the pie, there's no null result. One of the slices must be taken (even though one of them is "no drop"), and this is true of almost every enemy death in the game. The second property of this kind of randomness is that the more slices of pie there are, the lower the odds that the player will get any one of them. For example, if we add more options for the game to select from when loot is dropping, the chances of selecting any one of them *must* go down.[40]

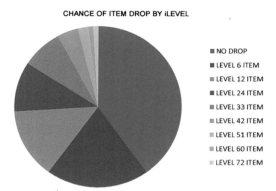

CHANCE OF ITEM DROP BY iLEVEL

■ NO DROP
■ LEVEL 6 ITEM
■ LEVEL 12 ITEM
■ LEVEL 24 ITEM
■ LEVEL 33 ITEM
■ LEVEL 42 ITEM
■ LEVEL 51 ITEM
■ LEVEL 60 ITEM
■ LEVEL 72 ITEM

This becomes an important dynamic in the late game, because higher-level enemies don't just drop high-level loot, they can also drop most of the loot below their level, too. Or, in other words, the *Diablo II* designers are always slicing the pie into smaller and smaller pieces, rather than simply changing the contents of each piece.

The third principle that makes the SOP randomness metaphor useful is that, when a slice of the pie grows or shrinks, other pieces of pie have to change as well. Why is this important to know? In *Diablo II*, the player has the power to change the sizes of the slices of pie. One of the most famous mechanics in *Diablo II* is its magic-find system through which the player can improve his or her odds of getting better items. Not only can the player make the size of the "rare" and "unique" pieces of pie, but by doing so they actually make the "normal" item slices (which are often useless) much smaller. We'll cover that portion of the system in detail, but it's also important to know that it's not the only place where the player can influence the size or number of slices. Indeed, the player can also change how many items drop, too, although the process requires other players and has some drawbacks.

Changing the Size and Number of Slices

The first thing that happens when items are being generated from corpses in *Diablo II* is a check that determines if any items drop at all. This is one of the easier places to start looking at how *Diablo II* generates items (and implements SOP randomness). When an enemy dies, the game rolls to see if an item drops. The no-drop slice of the pie is based on an area-wide variable rather than something in the monster itself. When the player is alone, the standard rate of "no drops" is about 62%. As more players enter the game and/or area where the current player is fighting, the no-drop rate decreases (Table 2.1).

Table 2.1 *Diablo II* No-Drop
Chances[41]

Players	No-Drop Chance (%)
1	62
2	48
3	24
4	14
5	9
6	4
7	3
8	1

Nothing within the game's UI explains that a greater number of players will see greater amounts of loot, although it makes intuitive sense. There needs to be more loot when there are more players so that everyone can have some! Just as players will notice that having more players around results in greater amounts of EXP filling up their level bar, players will also notice the greater amount of loot through what they see on the screen. *Diablo II* is infamous for all of its "junk" loot that nobody wants—low-level common items or broken versions of gear. Even though this gear is almost always useless, it works well as an indicator of the current local drop rate.

The no-drop calculation is only a part of the first step, and there are several SOP rolls that lead the game to its choice of item. One of the important properties of SOP randomness is that, as one slice of the pie shrinks, the others have to grow. What is growing when the no-drop slice shrinks? The other selections in the first step are large meta-tables—tables that contain other tables. In his excellent guide on magic find mechanics, Fendriradramelk examines some of these meta-tables, which I have reorganized and visualized below. When a player kills a skeleton on hell difficulty, it can drop the following (Table 2.2).

Table 2.2 Treasure Class (TC)
Chances—Act 1 (H) H2H A[42]

Probability	Contents (%)
No Drop	75
Gold	8.75
Act 1 (H) Equip A	6.66
Act 1 (H) Junk	8.75
Act 1 (H) Good	0.8

The meta-table descriptions are fairly accurate to what they contain. "Act 1 (H) Junk" drops junk and "Act 1 (H) Good" will drop fairly good items, relative to the level of the monster that drops them. "Act 1 (H) Equip A" is the one that players are really looking for, however; it has the useful gear that players need to improve their character. Unfortunately, the player has no influence over which one of these slices the game randomly chooses. More characters means a greater chance of loot dropping, but the newest and best loot doesn't replace the no-drop slice of pie at a 1:1 ratio. As the monsters increase in level, new slices are added to the pie in the form of new item tables, but this actually causes quite a few problems for players who are hunting for specific pieces of gear. As the second property of SOP randomness states, every new slice makes every other slice smaller. Moreover, the newest items are always added as the smallest slices. This is intentional; high-end items become extremely powerful on the later difficulties, and the designers have to maintain the game balance and give the players something to work towards. There are other bottlenecks in the SOP randomness method that appear to be unintentional. These problems tend to arise from the unequal distribution of items in different treasure classes. Below is a pie graph that displays just the set and unique items of treasure class (TC) 30, which drops from enemies around level 40.[43]

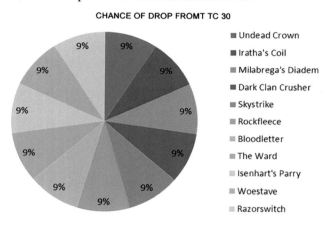

Once the item selection process reaches this step, there's a reasonable chance that a player will get the item they want, especially after multiple runs.[44]

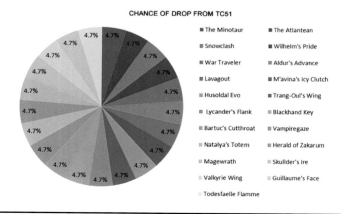

2. The Different Kinds of Randomness in *Diablo II*

Look at TC 51, here. The abundance of treasure in this treasure class means that even if the player manages to get a roll that selects TC 51, the likelihood of getting the actual item they want is significantly lower because there are so many slices of pie. This isn't the most common problem, but it does affect the player's chances of finding certain items in a way that probably wasn't intentional. The designers definitely wanted to minimize the drops of elite gear and did so successfully. Whether or not they wanted to minimize the chances of any one item in TC 51 is doubtful, and probably an oversight.

Economy Crunch

This problem of too many slices is magnified at the highest levels. As the game adds more and more slices to the pie of TCs that can drop, the chances of getting any individual piece of gear drop precipitously. For mid- and lower-level gear that still has high-level utility (some of which we'll see in Chapter 3), the player can eliminate some of these slices by targeting lower-level monsters. For elite gear, the player has no other option than to target monsters with the greatest number of slices in the hope that the elite slice will be chosen. To get a sense of how much less these items drop than items in earlier tiers, I have created a visualization of the drop rates of each successive TC.[45]

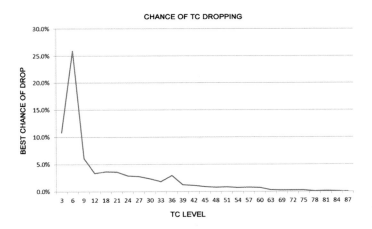

What you're seeing above is the rate at which a TC drops from the monster most likely to drop it. For example, Griswold is the monster most likely to drop TC six, and he drops an item from it roughly 25% of the time per pick when he dies on normal difficulty. Baal is the monster most likely to drop TC 87, but he only drops it 0.1% of the times he dies. (Note that I have multiplied by the standard number of drops that a monster has, which affects the final odds. Normal monsters have one or two drop slots, but boss monsters tend to drop four or more items if the drop slots don't have a no-drop result. Baal isn't the most likely to drop TC 87 per drop slot, but he is the most likely to drop it because he has so many slots.)

These drop rates mean that a player will only see, on average, one TC 87 item per one thousand times they kill Baal, and that's assuming that every single one of those Baal runs is completely full so that the no-drop rate is negligible—or else the odds are even worse! (Note that these are average odds. In my simulations of Baal runs, I routinely ran into stretches where a TC 87 item did not drop for two or three thousand kills in a row—something plenty of players have experienced.) If every game has to be full in order to achieve these odds, then there are going to be eight players competing for the same loot. *Diablo III* famously solved this problem by generating loot for each player separately, but we're studying the game that the designers made, not the one they wish they had made. The best items in *Diablo II* are rare, and players compete fiendishly for them. For his part, David Brevik said that he thought many items were a little too rare, especially the highest TCs and the rarest runes. He said he actually appreciated some of the events that *Diablo III* employed to increase drop rates for a limited time and/or under certain conditions.[46] In spite of all this, it's not as though *Diablo II* is unplayable because of this extreme difficulty. In section three of this book, we're going to see how even moderately powerful gear is still very useful, especially when part of a set, but we've still got a few forms of randomness to examine before we get there.

Magic Find and SOP Randomness

The last step that *Diablo II* performs when generating items is to determine the quality of the item—whether the item is normal, magic, rare, set, or unique. This is essentially the last pie in a long line of pies, but it's also the one the player has the most control over. The largest slice of the pie is normal items, but every enemy has an inherent chance of dropping a magic item. When the player equips gear with "% Better Chance of Getting Magic Item," they augment the drop rate from those monsters. There are two important things to know about this augmentation, as they relate to SOP randomness. First, all of the gains made are at the expense of the "normal items" slice. This is pretty obvious, because there's nothing else to take from.[47,48]

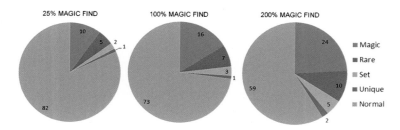

The tricky thing is that the best slices—set and unique items—grow much more slowly than the magic and rare slices. What's more, they receive diminishing

2. The Different Kinds of Randomness in *Diablo II*

benefits from magic find bonuses as the amount grows. In one way, this limits the amount of control the player has over the process; they can't ever really reach a point where unique or set items will always drop. In another way, the diminishing returns make the game more interesting in a way totally consistent with all the other stats. Attack speed, attack rating, casting speed, and move speed all incur significant diminishing returns as well. The purpose of that dynamic is to make the player take a more balanced approach to their character's stats. One of the things we'll see in Chapter 3 of this book is that players have more control over the rate at which they kill monsters than they do the amount of reward they get for doing so. Magic find helps a lot, and players should seek it out, but at the same time, they need to make sure their character is a worthy warrior.

Key Lessons about Slice-of-Pie Randomness

- Be careful about ever-expanding drop tables. If you keep adding slices to the pie, it will be less and less likely that the player will ever see the smallest slices.
- *Diablo II* gives the player the ability to directly and indirectly augment the size of slices (through magic find affixes and party sizes, respectively), and this was famously successful.
- The game doesn't give the player the power to add or subtract slices, however. This may have been the problem that led to some items being too rare.

Deck-of-Cards Randomness

The next two types of randomness overlap a lot, but there are some critical differences. The one I'm going to discuss here is what I call "deck of cards" (DOC) randomness. Almost everyone who can read English has encountered the 52-card deck, but even if you haven't, almost all card games operate by this principle. The most important quality of the 52-card deck—and really a deck in most card games—is that it contains repeats. There are four jacks, four sevens, etc. Thus, players have a 7.6% chance of getting any given type of card, but the repeats are limited, so when the jack of diamonds enters play, the chances that any other player will get a jack from the deck drops slightly. Professional card players have to be able to do this math in their heads in order to win consistently. There's a second important quality to DOC randomness that comes in at this point, however. Depending on the game that's being played, the deck is shuffled (randomized) at different intervals. In blackjack, there are often several decks being used, and professional card players need to know when a new (randomized) deck is being used, or when all the decks are re-randomized in order to win. The third important characteristic of DOC randomness is that the cards in it are interdependent in certain ways. In solitaire, for example, the player can only build columns of cards based on numerical order.

The part of the game that depends most on DOC randomness is map generation. Just above, we looked at how important objects on the map are placed by RR methods, but most of the work is done out of a deck of cards. The cards themselves are what level designer Stefan Scandizzo called "presets." Essentially, the computer draws from a deck of pre-made level chunks and fits them together. We'll examine this process through the lens of the DOC characteristics. Note that almost all the information below comes from my interview with Scandizzo, although the terms I use for randomness are original to this document.[49]

1. *Decks have repeats*: The computer draws cards from a deck of pre-made chunks and places them on the map. Although there are many repeats in the deck (connecting hallways being the most common type of repeat), the computer can only draw the same card so many times before a shuffle. This prevents dungeons from feeling like a total copy/paste job. This process is deceptively complex, however, because there are a huge number of cards in the deck, and they vary greatly.

2. *The deck gets re-randomized (shuffled)*: Certain parts of the map have much smaller decks (like zone border walls, pictured below) and therefore have more repeats. The borders of outdoor maps are particularly prone to this, and often experience "shuffling" more than other parts of the map. That said, the bigger a map is, the more often the player will see repeats. The level's preset decks are much larger than most people imagine, but they are ultimately limited and will recycle if they run out. This is probably the least important part of DOC randomness in the game, however, since most of the decks are quite large.

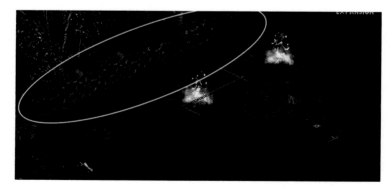

3. *The cards in the deck interact in specific ways*: Whether the preset card ends in an empty edge or an aperture like a doorway, it can only connect with another preset that can receive it. If the edges of the card drawn match the edges of the card previously laid down, it connects them. If not, it inserts them back into the deck. (This reinsertion is essentially a "soft shuffle.")

Examining the Cards

What does a card from the deck look like? It varies greatly. Some presets are only a few yards across and have one edge that can attach to another preset card—these are often dead ends. There are a lot of these cards, and the deck contains duplicates of some of them. Others are gigantic spaces with several branches, of which there is only one copy of this type of preset in the deck per dungeon.

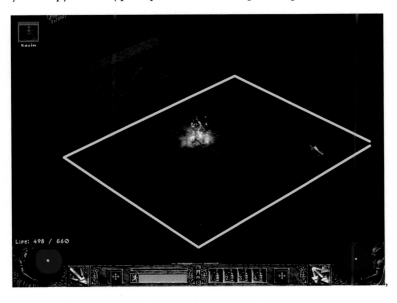

In the right hand screenshot, it's the mini-map that's important. The entire circled section is a single preset.[50] How can presets be so large if the dungeons are supposed to feel new each time? There are a few things affecting this, but the most important one is that there are dozens to hundreds of presets of varying sizes in each deck. Although neither I nor any of the people I interviewed had the means to count, you can understand how big some of the decks were by the time spent making them. Stefan Scandizzo was one of three level designers, and he spent nearly three years of full time labor making presets.[51] Although algorithms are a great productivity tool, they're only as useful as the assets they draw upon.

Because of the above, the structure and feel of *Diablo II* dungeons actually depends more on the nature and number of cards in the preset deck than any quirk of the procedural algorithm. Dungeons gain their flavor from the shape of the presets. Narrow, winding presets like those in the Maggot Lair make it feel claustrophobic and difficult to navigate. (Scandizzo actually said he spent a ton of time on this dungeon, and was surprised to learn of its poor reputation among veteran players.[52]) The contrast between huge rooms and narrow apertures in the Durance of Hate can make it feel like the player is suddenly dropped into a trap. The many similar forks in caves like the Underground Passage can make it feel like the player has been wandering endlessly with no sign of an exit. The algorithms for each dungeon and outdoor zone are slightly different; both Scandizzo and Brevik confirmed this. Nevertheless, it's the pieces of each zone that make the magic happen.

Although enemy and treasure placement do not technically use DOC randomness, they are still connected to the structure of presets and fairly simple in execution. On each preset, there are several pre-programmed "receptors" upon which enemies and treasure can be placed.

2. The Different Kinds of Randomness in *Diablo II*

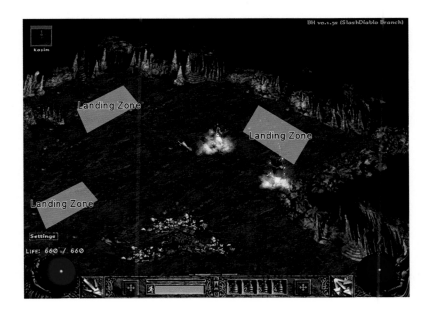

Once the map has been fully generated, the game places enemies on these receptors in waves. Each preset has a maximum density of enemies. Although none of the devs I interviewed remembered the formula exactly, it appears that the density calculation isn't entirely dependent on the raw number of enemies. Some types of enemies have several sizes of "pack" to pick from.[53] Those packs have varying weights based on the number and type of monsters in them. The game places a wave of random packs (of various sizes) on the map. Then, for every preset that isn't over its maximum weight, more packs are added until the predefined population is reached.[54-56] The same process then repeats for treasure chests, which are distributed according to density limits on the receptors that can hold them. These packs and treasure chests can be (and frequently are) repeated over and over again if the computer chooses them randomly, so they don't follow the DOC randomness guidelines.

Not every preset has an equal number of receptors, and not all receptors are equal. One of the few things about map generation that veteran players did know was that there are many chests and locations where a special chest or monster would reliably appear. In other words, there are map presets which also come with chest presets. The chests around the small bonfire in Lower Kurast are a good example, and are a favorite target of master item hunters. The lesson to be extracted from this is that procedural generation has its limits, both in technological and artistic terms. If the game is too random, long-time players won't experience as much of a payoff for mastering the game. If the game relies too much on preconstructed material, then it is too easily optimized and just becomes a math problem with no surprises. The tension between randomness and familiarity is what makes *Diablo II* the game it is.

Key Lessons in Deck of Cards Randomness

- The most important part of DOC randomness is the number and variety of cards in the deck. Without dozens or hundreds of cards, dungeons will get a copy/paste feel very quickly.
- Just as the cards in solitaire or poker have matching numbers and suits for ordering the gameplay, so do the cards in the map generation deck have matching edges and apertures for making sensible architecture.
- Although the cards themselves are one layer of randomness, there's another layer of randomness in the "hot spots" on the cards.
- The cards are randomly placed from the deck, but sometimes the cards have fixed features, like special treasure chests, which experienced players can seek out.

Set Randomness

The last kind of randomness at work in *Diablo II* is what I call set randomness. There's a lot of overlap between set randomness and DOC randomness. For example, the odds of getting the right item change as the player draws more items from the deck (or bag, or loot table). Indeed, you could say from a mathematical perspective that set randomness and DOC randomness are the same thing, but for the purpose of game design I think it's helpful to look at them through different lenses. Set randomness deals with sets that are built over longer periods of time. Although the players in a round of poker are trying to complete a set like a straight, they're done with the hand after a few minutes, and the value of their sets is totally dependent on the other sets in play. Moreover, In DOC randomness, all cards are equally likely to be played. In set randomness, some pieces of a set are more common than others. A better illustration of set randomness comes from the tabletop game *Scrabble*. In *Scrabble*, players draw random letters to try to complete words, but the letters aren't all equally common. Overall, this type of randomness has four essential characteristics, as it applies to *Diablo II*. Although some of these characteristics overlap with DOC randomness, I repeat them with a different example, because it's helpful to understand the concept from another perspective.

1. *The player selects pieces randomly, but the pieces are much more valuable when they form sets.* For example, "Z" is a great letter to pick randomly in Scrabble because it's worth 10 points, but the player only gets those points if they can form an English word like "zoo" or "quiz." *Diablo II* is a little more lenient; runes and set items that drop randomly can be valuable by themselves. That said, they are much, much more valuable as part of a set. (This rule overlaps with DOC randomness.)

2. *Pieces can be part of more than one set.* Just as the letters "T" and "Y" can be part of the words "try," "toy" or "stay," so too can pieces in *Diablo II* be

2. The Different Kinds of Randomness in *Diablo II*

part of more than one set. Runes can obviously be part of several different runewords. "Ber" is part of the runewords "Enigma" and "Beast," for example. Denoted or "green" set items are also part of multiple sets. By the rules of *Diablo*, all the items in the Sigon's Complete Steel set are part of one set.

Partial Set Bonus

+10% Life Stolen Per Hit (2 Items)

+100 Defense (3 Items)

Complete Set Bonus

+10% Life Stolen Per Hit

+100 Defense

+20 To Mana

Fire Resist +12%

+24 To Max Fire Damage

Attacker Takes Damage of 12

Damage Reduced By 7

When all of the items in the set are equipped, the player gains quite a few bonuses, but when just a few items are equipped, the player is able to gain partial bonuses. These partial bonuses (there are several different levels of them) are each a set nested within the larger "named" set of Sigon's Complete Steel. (This, too, can overlap with DOC randomness; hands of poker also work this way.)

3. *Not all parts of a set are equally common.* This is where set randomness diverges from DOC randomness in an important way. If a player randomly draws the Q in Scrabble, waiting for a U tile is a prudent move, because there are four U tiles (and two blanks, which serve just as well). On the other hand, a player with the U tile would be crazy to wait for the Q, since there's only one Q tile in the game. Similarly, players in *Diablo II* who happen to get the amulet Tal Rasha's Horadric Crest have gotten the "Q" of that set, and would be wise to keep an eye out for the rest of it. The belt from that same set, Tal-Rasha's Wrappings, is relatively common and shouldn't change the player's farming behavior. This is important in *Diablo II* because inventory space is limited. With a limited amount of inventory and stash space to put objects, players have to be somewhat selective about what they're picking up. (Even players who have numerous mules to hold their gear still have to go through the annoying process of managing them all.) As they gain experience,

players will begin to notice which items tell them that they should collect the rest of a set.

4. *As players collect pieces of a set, the chance that they will get the remaining pieces drops.* Let's say a Scrabble player wants to spell the word "judge" when they draw their first seven letters. Assuming they are the first person to draw letters, they have a 25% chance of drawing any of the five letters in the word "judge." (There are 100 letters in the bag, including duplicates, and 25 of them are in the word judge.) Let's say the player gets everything but the G in the first four letters he draws. The chance of drawing the G would only be 3.125%. (There are 96 letters left in the bag and three of them are Gs.) This is just because the chances of drawing a G are always going to be lower than the combined chances of drawing a J, U, D, or E.

When a player in *Diablo II* collects his or her first item in a set, the odds of collecting another missing piece of that set are relatively high, especially if the set has a large number of pieces. The odds of any single monster dropping a set item are small, but across thousands of monster kills, the player will see some set items. If the chances of any piece of the set are roughly equal, the chance of a new item dropping in a desired set is relatively high, but once the player already has a bunch of items, it's likely that he or she will see duplicate drops as often as new drops. Although the player seeks to complete sets, the system that distributes set items provides them in no particular order.

Key Lessons about Set Randomness

- Set randomness is similar to DOC randomness, but with a few important differences.
- Sets are more powerful than the sum of their components.
- Not all parts of a set are equally common, so there are certain pieces of a set that indicate the whether player should start collecting or not.
- No matter how common set items are, the player will have a harder time finding the last piece of the set than the first piece of it.

Reflecting on Randomness in *Diablo II*

Randomness is a toolkit, not a tool. There are many different ways to implement randomness, and *Diablo II* uses quite a few of them. The key to understanding *Diablo*-style randomness is to understand that it draws upon ideas which were already at play in many different kinds of games. From solitaire to *Scrabble*, there are many different ways of shaping randomness so that human players can strategize, influence, and control it, while still being occasionally surprised by it. One of the great delights of *Diablo II* is finding a powerful item at random. One of the great frustrations of *Diablo II* is being unable to complete a set of great items. Both of these things keep people playing, and as they understand more about the game and its systems, they appreciate the game more. I think that state of being thrilled by a game even as it lays its own bones bare to you is one of the hallmarks of depth. Nearly 20 years later, it seems like *Diablo II* nailed depth through randomness in items, maps, and monsters, or we wouldn't still be talking about it or returning to it quite so often.

3

Schaefer Variation and Acceleration Flow

This chapter of the book deals with the idiosyncratic design structure of *Diablo II*, an idea I call Schaefer variation. In this chapter, we will examine what Schaefer variation is, how it is implemented, and what effect this has on the player's experience of *Diablo II*. The shortest explanation of Schaefer variation is that it is a way of recreating the fundamental design structure of mainstream action games in a procedural RPG. To explain this, this chapter of the book will synthesize information from the first two chapters to explain how this effect is achieved. In addition, this chapter of the book will also cover a directly related phenomenon I call acceleration flow. Acceleration flow is not a design dynamic, but rather a psychological experience that a player can have in RPGs. Acceleration flow is a state of focused euphoria that results from changes in the rate at which a player-character gains levels. We'll examine that phenomenon and how Schaefer variation contributes to it naturally.

Breaking Out of the RPG Straightjacket

Many of the design dynamics in *Diablo II* seem to be constructed to keep the difficulty the same at all times. At first glance, this seems like it is incompatible with a phenomenon that has the word "variation" right in it. For example, one of the most obvious over-arching dynamics in *Diablo II* is its level-deterministic zones. That is, monsters in a given zone have a base level, and they don't really vary from that level unless they spawn as champion or unique monsters. Even then, the variation in monster level is minimal. The monsters in the Tamoe Highland on Nightmare difficulty, for example, are level 39. Champions in that zone are level 41. Uniques in that zone are level 42. All of the damage, HP, defense, attack rating, and EXP values in that zone are a product of monster level and monster type (and procedural affixes, if the monster has any). For the most part, all of the zones in *Diablo II* increase in level in a linear way.[57]

Diablo II **Monster Level by Zone**

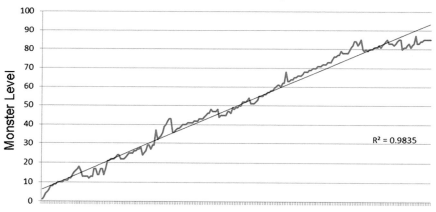

Successive Zones (3 Difficulty Settings)

Most of the steeper rises in the graph are in act five of each difficulty setting, but there aren't any major peaks or valleys at all across the rest of the game. The r-squared value does illustrate how linear monster level is across the mandatory zones of the game.

Does the linear shape of *Diablo's* level determinism mean that the difficulty of the game is almost always exactly the same? No, and there are several reasons why. The first is that the game is an action RPG, so enemy level doesn't always tell you everything. Enemies also have action-game attributes that can make them harder or easier to kill. Run speed, projectile speed, and sprite size are three dimensions that are not always balanced in accordance with monster level.

3. Schaefer Variation and Acceleration Flow

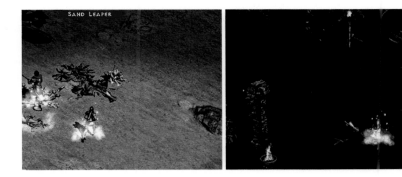

Enemies like the Leaper and Fetish all move quickly, relative to a normal-speed character. They do less-than-normal damage for the areas in which they appear, but the player has a harder time avoiding or escaping them. Incautious players can easily find themselves swarmed by huge packs of these monsters and unable to lose them, especially when their character's stamina runs out. Nowhere is this worse than in the jungles of Act 3, in which large numbers of Fetishes can rapidly fire dozens of projectiles which move fast and are often hard to see against the background color of the map. Trying to hit these small, fast-moving enemies can be equally frustrating; even clicking their sprites can sometimes be difficult. Players with great defense stats or tremendous damage output can overcome these problems to some degree. But that still means that these zones are harder than their level might suggest.

Map generation is another area in which it's possible for procedural generation to yield a sudden spike in difficulty without any unusual changes to monster stats. As we saw in the map generation section in Chapter 2, every map card in the procedural deck has several possible landing spots for procedurally generated enemies. Although there are maximum population limits for each landing spot and for the map as a whole, no part of the algorithm guarantees an even distribution of enemies.

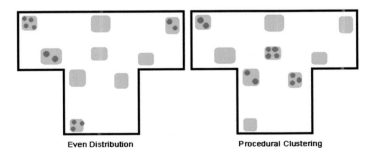

Even Distribution   Procedural Clustering

If the enemy distribution algorithm happens to place enemies in a cluster on the map, the game can suddenly become more difficult for certain types of characters.

This effect is magnified if one or more of those enemies is a unique monster with special affixes. A large crowd backed by a unique monster and his elite pack greatly increases the damage and danger they can output. This is especially true if one or more of the unique monsters has an aura affix, directly augmenting all of the nearby monsters. Under these conditions, a moderately difficult cluster of packs can become quite vicious, and often even the best players will reload their game to clear it.

Of course, there are also places where the game gets easier through procedural means as well. Sometimes, there is an enemy who is weak to the player's build, or one that has a behavior that the player can exploit. Sometimes greater ease comes from an item drop or a new ability that gives the player a surge in power. The important thing to know about *Diablo II* is that there are many peaks and valleys in the difficulty of the game, despite the constant level determinism. The surges in power are a little more important, psychologically, than the surges in difficulty, but we'll take a look at both in this next section.

Bosses, Behavior, and the Organic Acceleration

Act bosses are a great place to examine both peaks and valleys in difficulty, and how both of those things are created by the game's mechanics. By one definition, act bosses are clearly harder than the rest of the content of the game. Act bosses are usually about 10 levels higher than the zones they inhabit, in addition to having tons of extra HP and many deadly attacks. To offset this, bosses also yield significantly greater rewards. Not only is act boss EXP usually about 40 times higher than normal enemy EXP at the same level,[58] but bosses also have a higher number of maximum (and average) drops per kill. Moreover, bosses are more likely to drop magical, rare, set, and unique items than common monsters. Although bosses are more difficult in one sense of the word, players don't always think of boss fights as making the overall game "harder" in the same way a jungle full of Fetishes shooting darts makes the game harder.

This brings up an important point about the perception of difficulty in RPGs. Players of RPGs do not necessarily think of the difficulty of the game as being only a product of how hard it is to kill individual monsters. Rather, players perceive the difficulty of an RPG to have to do more with the ratio of rewards over time, what I'll call the R/T ratio from now on. *Diablo II's* act bosses are obviously much tougher than regular monsters, but they provide such a large amount of reward that the R/T ratio doesn't decrease. (The numerator in this ratio can be any kind of reward, like EXP, gear, runes, gems or gold, or any combination of those things.) Indeed, the ratio might actually increase when a player figures out how to handle a boss's behavior patterns or finds a build that allows them to quickly dispose of a particular boss.

The situation described in the paragraph above is what I call an organic acceleration. Any time a player can isolate a specific part of an RPG (like a certain dungeon or specific enemy) and exploit a strategy to raise the R/T ratio, they are in an acceleration. The organic acceleration depends entirely on behavior and exists in almost all digital RPGs. Almost all RPG designers want their players to find ways to be better at the game. Thus, when a player learns how to exploit the weakness of a boss or masters the use of a new ability, they're doing something the designer intended for them to do, which is why I call behavior-based accelerations organic. An acceleration of this kind looks something like this:

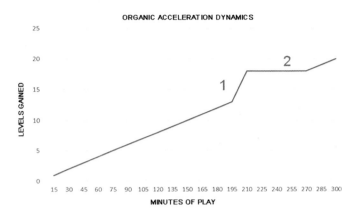

The acceleration is the sharp increase in slope marked by the number one on the graph. The player's newly devised (or discovered) strategy doesn't actually increase the reward in the R/T ratio. He's fighting the same enemies, and they offer the same rewards. Instead, the player's strategy drives down the time denominator by exploiting some feature of the game design. (Later on, we'll see how *Diablo II* allows players to drive up the reward numerator as well.)

There's another important bit of information on the graph above: after an organic acceleration, there's a corresponding deceleration that happens immediately afterwards. Almost all organic accelerations have the corresponding deceleration, because their primary reward is experience points. (You can see the deceleration marked by the number two on the graph above.) When a player uses an organic acceleration to gain a few levels in quick succession, he actually devalues the rewards of the next few areas or dungeons. Whenever a player enters a new dungeon at a higher level than necessary, the EXP rewards will seem relatively smaller. In *Diablo II*, this effect is magnified because players are penalized for killing lower-level enemies. This deceleration can sometimes be so frustrating that it spoils the euphoria that the player was experiencing during the acceleration. Advanced players often skip the decelerated part of the curve by running through certain zones. By the mid-2000s, experienced *Diablo II* players were often accelerating in a few key spots, like Tristram, the Tombs, Throne of Destruction, etc. and not even engaging with the rest of the game's content. Before that became a widespread practice, the deceleration was a widely-experienced downside to the organic acceleration, and it was meant to be that way because the *Diablo II* designers had something else in mind for bigger and less frustrating accelerations.

Bosses, Behavior, and the Organic Acceleration

Schaefer Variation in Microcosm

The organic acceleration presents a problem for the thesis of Chapter 3 of this book. How can I claim that *Diablo II* benefits from accelerations and acceleration flow if the resulting decelerations cancel them out? The answer is that there is more than one kind of acceleration, and Schaefer variation provides a kind of acceleration with a softer landing, so to speak. If the organic acceleration is the basic model of accelerations in general, the unique weapon drop is the basic model of Schaefer variation. Let's say that a level 24 Paladin clears the River of Flame, and one of the monsters there drops the unique grand scepter Rusthandle. That Paladin is currently using a magical (blue) weapon of significantly less power than the unique drop. Suddenly, that Paladin is a lot more powerful, and can kill enemies at a significantly faster rate. Thus, the R/T ratio grows in the player's favor.

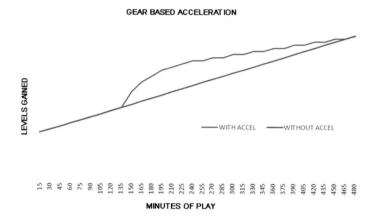

The important difference in this graph is that there's no corresponding deceleration. Instead, the acceleration slowly falls off until the R/T ratio returns to its most common value. From the Paladin's perspective, Rusthandle is extremely powerful at first, and helps him to smash through enemies at a rate which is much higher than normal. He doesn't have to stop and exploit a single zone. The power of the unique mace can carry him through several consecutive zones quickly, collecting EXP and item drops at an enhanced rate the whole way. As he gets deeper into the game, however, the relative power of Rusthandle diminishes until it's at the level of something the player could find in a shop. At that point, the R/T ratio returns to its base rate and the acceleration is over. It is this type of acceleration which makes *Diablo II* the game it is.

Diablo II also has idiosyncratic spikes in difficulty. The important thing to remember about the game is that Schafer variation depends on procedural means. Rusthandle dropped for our hypothetical Paladin as a random drop. No enemy in the game is guaranteed to drop it and give the player an acceleration. By the same token, there are plenty of instances when an extra-powerful monster spawns and gives the player a bigger challenge. The power of monsters is relative to the character who tries to kill them. Barbarians don't worry too much about unique monsters with the "Extra Fast" affix; they're going to be surrounded by enemies anyway. If a Barbarian encounters an enemy with the Stone Skin affix (which confers physical resistance), it will give him a little more trouble. Similarly, the Sorceress doesn't care about Stone Skin since she only deals elemental damage, but the extra fast monsters make it hard for her to stay at range, where she's safe. Regardless of the class, however, all players will eventually encounter monster packs that are especially difficult for their character.

The result of these procedurally generated super-monsters and procedurally dropped super-weapons pushing the difficulty is Schafer variation. Across the course of the game, the player will kill thousands of monsters and encounter hundreds of procedurally generated packs of extra-powerful enemies. With all those chances for something to go either very right or very wrong for the player, the landscape of difficulty looks something like this:

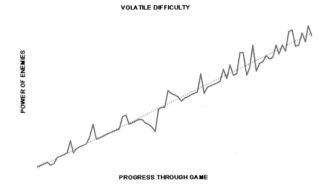

In this graph, I have tried to represent the volatility of Schaefer variation by spacing the peaks and valleys unevenly. In reality, those peaks and valleys could be anywhere, but they're definitely a part of the experience of *Diablo II*. Now, let's bring back the original graph of what Nishikado motion looks like.

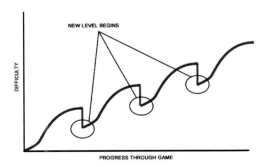

Schafer variation is volatile in a way that Nishikado motion usually isn't, but the general structure is the same. There's also another attribute that Schaefer variation and Nishikado motion have in common. Over time, both traditional action games and *Diablo II* gradually become more difficult. The next section examines how this happens because the process is actually much more complex than it seems. Indeed, all explanations of *how* things happen in game design are more complex than explanations of *what* things happens in game design, but the how of game design is usually more interesting—and *Diablo II* is no exception.

Historical Note on Schaefer Variation

Before moving on to the next section, I want to address an issue in the history of RPG design. Why does Schaefer variation exist in the first place? Why do RPGs need to emulate an action game difficulty structure? The tabletop RPGs from which *Diablo II* is descended don't frequently employ major variations or accelerations in the same way a game like *Diablo II* does. It would be difficult for them to do so because those games proceed much more slowly than computer RPGs. Even if they did exist in tabletop form, accelerations would be hard to perceive; even relatively small tabletop battles can take thirty minutes to finish. Another reason that tabletop games don't have accelerations is that they're built with adaptive difficulty in mind. In a well-run tabletop session, the dungeon or game master will constantly adjust the difficulty of the game to keep players on their toes. Digital RPGs can't really replicate the dynamic difficulty of a tabletop game. No computer program can match a good DM's ability to read his or her players and the situation they find themselves in. Given this inability, it shouldn't be surprising that digital RPGs borrowed the (extremely successful) difficulty structure that emerged from console action games. The oldest theme in videogame design is that technological constraints become artistic strategies. Thus, a lack of dynamic difficulty gradually gave rise to the incorporation of videogame-style difficulty peaks and valleys and the accelerations they sometimes yield.

Long-Term Difficulty and Planned Deficits

If *Diablo's* primary characteristics are procedural swings in difficulty and level-deterministic zones, how can the game become more difficult over time? The most obvious way would be for the procedural spikes in difficulty to become more frequent, and that does happen. The game is designed so that there will be more chances for procedural peaks in difficulty in the later difficulties (mostly by spawning more unique monsters). The designers do not only rely on random peaks; they also raise the base difficulty of the game so that the valleys in between the peaks will be more difficult as the player gets deeper into the game. But still—how is this possible with the strict level determinism we've already seen? The answer is that in *Diablo II*, the value of character levels gradually diminishes across the course of the game.

I call this design dynamic a *planned deficit*. To give a simple example of the idea, I'll borrow from another genre. In many settlement/city-building simulation games, designers use planned deficits to cause crises for the player to solve. For example, in *Sim City 2000*, the power plants introduced in the first 50 years of game time are less and less efficient (than plants introduced later) in terms of megawatts per dollar. This single design decision accomplishes a lot, however.

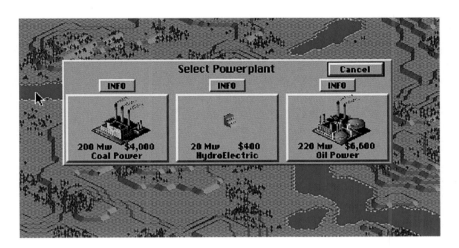

For one thing, it prevents players from expanding too rapidly in the early part of the game, since the return on investment from available power plants is too low. This is good, because it prevents the player from completely filling the map before all the later building options become available. The deficit also forces players to take a more analytical approach to their spending. It's easier to buy a gas power plant and save space, but the megawatt/dollar returns are lower. Then, later in the game, the player can get the best levels of efficiency from the microwave and nuclear power plants, but they have to deal with the high startup costs and plan accordingly. By deliberately building in a power deficit, the designers create inherent problems which the player has to solve throughout the game. Although these problems require testing and balancing (as all parts of every game do), they nevertheless show that the planned deficit is a useful tool in the game designer's kit.

Diablo II uses planned deficits as well, although it implements them in a different context. In *Diablo II*, the player-character's natural stats—the HP, dexterity, skill levels, and other stats obtained through levels and not through gear—are enough to carry him or her through the first difficulty setting. Although all characters should upgrade their gear whenever they can, the first difficulty setting is easy enough that the player rarely has to stop and grind for gear or EXP. Buying the best gear available in the town shop is often good enough to push through all the normal content. On the second difficulty setting, however, the player will gradually find that gear from the shop combined with the character's natural stats aren't quite as strong as they used to be. Especially for inexperienced players, this will cause quite a few more deaths than the last difficulty. The player will also notice they actually level up slower than before.[59]

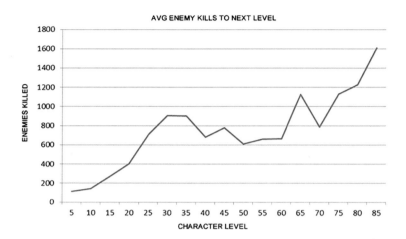

In terms of the raw number of monsters a player has to kill and overall time, the R/T ratio drops a lot as the player hits the final difficulty setting. Not only will the player spend more actual time earning each level, but the R/T ratio also decreases to emphasize the player's perception of that fact.

The decrease in the relative amount of EXP a player receives is only the beginning of the planned deficits that appear in *Diablo II*. As players make their way through the game, they will notice that it becomes harder to kill enemies and survive, because of a variety of stat deficits. The major deficits are:

Offensive Deficits
- The player damage deficit
- The attack rating deficit

Defensive Deficits
- The HP deficit
- Armor/block deficits
- Elemental resistance deficit

Although these all seem obvious, the degree of the deficit and the means of its construction are more complex than one might expect. We'll take a look at how each deficit is created and balanced in the following section.

The Damage Deficit

As the game goes on, the player does less damage to enemies, relative to how much HP those enemies have. There are two causes of the damage deficit. The first is the explosion in enemy HP, which is visualized on the in the following graph.[60]

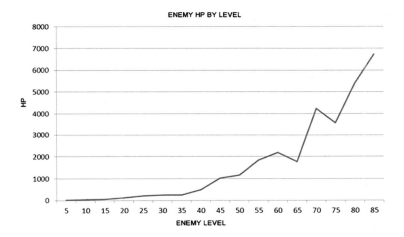

Late in the game, especially on the final difficulty setting, enemy HP starts to climb much faster than it did before. Enemy HP increases quite drastically and weapon DPS simply doesn't keep up. The next graph on this page visualizes how long it would take to kill the average monster with a one-handed weapon with the best magical (blue) affix available at the current level, demonstrating how later weapons aren't sufficient.[61]

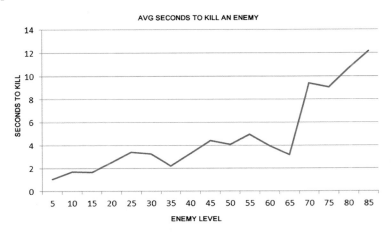

Long-Term Difficulty and Planned Deficits

(Although more difficult to visualize like this, the damage enhancement from caster weapons follows a similar trend.) Experienced players of *Diablo II* might object: "pure damage affixes aren't the only way to increase DPS!" That's absolutely true. There are other affixes that add elemental damage, attack speed, maximum or minimum damage, etc. Getting gear with all of those stats, however, requires the player to spend extra time farming. That slows the game down and makes it feel harder because the principle part of the R/T ratio (EXP) drops even more than it already has.

The second major factor in the damage deficit is the increasing prevalence of elemental resistances (including resistance to physical damage). On the hardest difficulty setting, enemies all gain substantial resistance to one or more elements, including physical damage. On top of the trend of already-inflated HP pools, these resistances inflate enemy HP even further. Why not just make enemy HP totals higher instead of making enemies resistant? The reason is that *Diablo II* is designed so that resistances can be solved orthogonally. If an enemy has no resistance and tons of HP, the only way to defeat that enemy quickly is to increase the player's damage output. If an enemy has a normal amount of HP and a high resistance to a certain element, the player has a variety of options. The player can switch elements. As we saw in the previous chapter, all the classes have access to at least two elements. *Diablo II* also gives players ways of mitigating resistances. Whether it's through active abilities (Amplify Damage, Lower Resist), passive abilities (Cold Mastery), or through gear which reduces enemy resistance directly (Facets, Tal Rasha's Lidless Eye), there are orthogonal means of beating resistance. Depending on the monster, these means are often much easier to obtain than a commensurate increase in direct damage output.

Regardless of how it's accomplished, many players find the drastic inflation of enemy HP to be the worst form of difficulty, as it is often time consuming without being more interesting. *Diablo II* isn't really guilty of turning enemies into "bullet sponges" in the traditional sense, however. *Diablo II* requires the player to slaughter thousands of enemies across the course of the game, often at a rate of more than one a second. Because the enemies on the first difficulty setting die so quickly, many of them don't even get a chance to attack. Increasing their HP allows normal enemies to survive long enough to get a shot off and pose a real threat. Under threat, the player has to use their defensive and mobility skills, making the game more interesting. Moreover, the increased threat of damage means that the player has to invest in defensive stats on their gear as well. As we'll see in the next section, that's an important part of late-game acceleration dynamics.

Attack Rating Deficit

Although all enemies gain one type of elemental immunity on the hardest difficulty, physical immunity is the second-least common type, at only 5% of all immune monsters. This is probably because most physical skills are already hampered by hit rating. There is a hit rating deficit which emerges across the course of the game, although it's not nearly as large as some of the other deficits, and it primarily affects melee characters when they face bosses (and Bowazons a lot more). The following graph visualizes hit rates by an average character against an average enemy with an average amount of dexterity and the best available weapon affix for attack rating.[62,63]

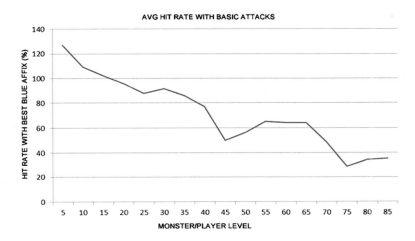

Of course, we also have to take into account the attack rating bonus that weapon-using characters gain from their skills. This bonus is often copious. Below, I have visualized the impact of the Barbarian's weapon mastery skills.[64]

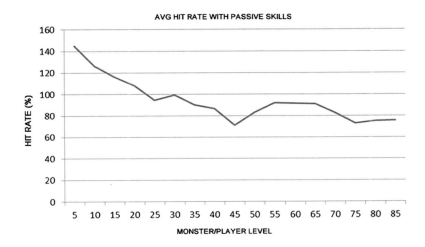

Most of the better passive skills triple the attacking character's AR with proper investment, and endgame combat skills commonly add another 200%–300% to it. (These bonuses are almost always additively applied). All of these combine to neutralize most of the attack rating deficit.

There are still a few things to consider about the hit rating deficit, however. First, while melee classes can get to about 75% hit rate with just their passive skills, spell casters always hit as long as the spell animation hits the enemy sprite. Second, attack skills often get the player close to maximum hit rating (95%), but enemies can still block. Third, the character will almost always have a higher deficit against bosses than they do against common enemies. A character hitting normal enemies at 90% will hit *Diablo* or Baal at a much lower rate. Those bosses have higher levels, better armor ratings, and better block rates. Any melee character looking to farm bosses will still have to use lots attack rating gear. As we saw earlier, attack rating incurs diminishing returns in large quantities. Just below, I have brought back and expanded the graph from part one, which shows the chances of hitting a monster of the same level as the character as attack rating increases.[65]

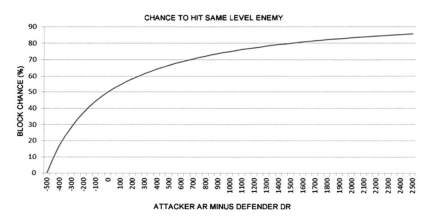

Players gain a ton of benefit from AR if their hit rate is low, but gain very little if their hit rate is high. This makes it difficult for characters that only use attacks to be able to stack hit rating at the highest levels, a disadvantage that spellcasters do not face. This curve also makes it difficult to precisely calculate the value of a quantity of attack rating; the amount is always changing. Further on in the level equivalency calculations, I will point out when AR is a huge factor in the power of a piece of gear because of this dynamic.

Armor and Block Deficits

The armor deficit is a little more complicated than the other deficits because it necessarily involves a large number of items. A character's armor rating is made up of the sum of all their armor: chest, helm, gloves, belt, boots, and shield. It's never easy to find a single item with the best possible affix, but trying to find five or six items with the best possible affixes is exceedingly difficult. Set randomness makes it hard to find every piece of any set, let alone sets of the best available defense affix at the character's current level. Accordingly, I have visualized both the armor value obtained from the best magical items, as well as the armor value obtained from gear with an affix half as powerful as the best one available.[66,67]

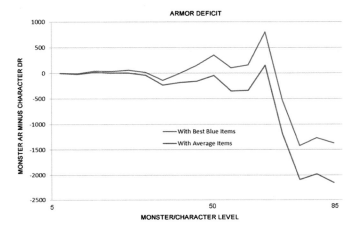

Note that the graph charts the difference between enemy AR and character defense, so that plunge into the negatives means the player is at a deficit. As you can see, the best magical items don't lift the player much above 50% at any time, and by the last difficulty setting, they are totally inadequate. Indeed, by level 85, even the best unique armor in the game isn't sufficient to match the hit rating of enemies (3313 armor vs 3971 average hit rating).[68] For the melee classes, abilities like Defiance or Iron Skin would put them over the halfway mark, but for casters the armor deficit is a more difficult problem to solve.

Part of the solution for every class is the use of a shield, which confers a separate form of evasion called blocking. Many characters can equip a shield to trade some damage for safety. Earlier, we saw that block goes down as level rises, unless the player invests heavily in dexterity.[69]

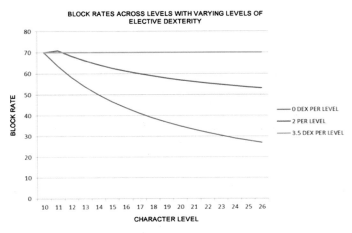

Characters that are built with tons of dexterity will block well throughout the game, but there's another factor to consider: the base block rate on shields maxes out at about 50%. The best affixes can bring this up to 70%. From this base amount, most melee classes can reach a 75% block rate without a superlative amount of dexterity. For them, there is one stat that doesn't incur a planned deficit. For the caster classes, block rate does drop quite a bit in the later game, making them more vulnerable. It's not surprising that the melee classes have better block rates, but it does show that casters have to deal with another planned deficit to make up for their ranged powers.

The HP Deficit

Although it seems like it should be the most straightforward form of deficit, the player-character HP deficit is much more complex than it seems. The simplest way to measure of the player-character HP deficit is to calculate the number of times the average enemy would need to hit the player-character to kill him or her.[70,71]

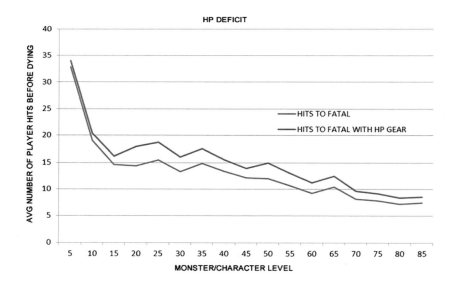

Over time, enemy damage outpaces average character HP growth. If we look at enemy damage by itself, the trend seems even more straightforward—and boring.[72]

3. Schaefer Variation and Acceleration Flow

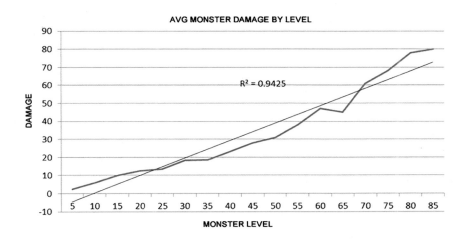

AVG MONSTER DAMAGE BY LEVEL

$R^2 = 0.9425$

Damage growth appears to be a function of the linear level-determinism of *Diablo II* and nothing more, but this is not the whole story. If we examine the growth of enemy damage as a percent instead of an absolute number, a different trend emerges.[73]

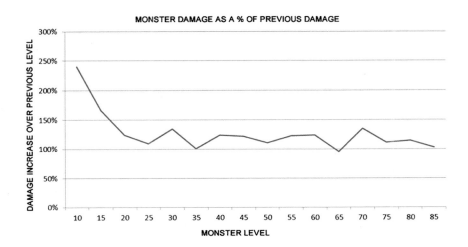

MONSTER DAMAGE AS A % OF PREVIOUS DAMAGE

Although the absolute damage of enemy attacks grows at a steady pace, the rate of the growth actually flattens out after the first difficulty setting. Compare this to the growth of enemy HP, which rises almost exponentially on the final difficulty setting, and it's clear that the designers had a clear idea of how to construct difficulty. This dynamic is even clearer when you look back at the relative amount of HP the best HP modifier affords the player in the first graph. The HP deficit is constructed to be smaller than the damage deficit. Players have to hunt a whole set of great items make up for the deficit in both areas, but it's supposed to be easier to make up the former. The designers don't want the player to die all the time; they want the biggest hurdle to be killing enemies.

There is another way in which the HP deficit is more forgiving than the damage deficit, and it serves as a good example of the design principles that shape endgame gear. One affix commonly found on higher level weapons is the "% Life Stolen Per Hit," commonly referred to as "lifesteal" or "life leech." This stat effectively makes the HP pool larger, as it constantly restores HP to characters when they strike the enemy. (This is one of the few stats that only benefits physical attacks rather than spells.) It's not really possible to make Lifesteal equivalent to a definite amount of HP, but the existence of an orthogonal means of increasing character HP shows us again how the designers intended players to acquire more power.

Solving the Deficits: Unique Items and LEQ

Everyone who has played *Diablo II* knows that powerful gear is at the heart of the game. Reading this analysis, you have probably guessed that the purpose of the many planned deficits is to force the player into finding gear. That is absolutely correct. What this section studies is how gear fills that gap because the most important thing in game design is not in the broad ideas, but in the execution of those ideas. What we see in *Diablo II* is that there is no one way to create a powerful item. Indeed, the variety of ways in which *Diablo II* allows players to become absurdly powerful is one of its greatest accomplishments.

Measuring Power with LEQ

Although *Diablo II* offers a great variety of powers to its players through gear, we still need to be able to assess those powers quantitatively. To do this, I use a statistic called level equivalency, or LEQ. One of the defining features of an RPG is that its characters gain levels, and gaining levels grants characters new powers. In a game like *Diablo II*, in which every character level is equally valuable in an absolute sense, we can use those levels as a unit of measurement to determine how specific abilities or pieces of gear compare to others. For example, when a character gains a level in *Diablo II*, how much health do they gain? We can use this amount of health as a measuring stick, so to speak. Let's take a look at the process of figuring out how much HP is equivalent to one character level.

1. First, we'll establish that when a character gains a "level" of HP, it means the player invests the five elective stat points into the HP stat, vitality.
2. Second, we need to use a "neutral" or average character. Instead of picking one character class, we'll take the median amount of HP a character can

gain. A median character gains two HP per level, plus three HP per stat point invested in vitality.

3. If our neutral character invests five points in vitality, and each is point is worth three HP, that's 15 HP. Add in two more HP that the character gets automatically at every level, and we know what a level of HP is worth to a neutral character: 17 HP.

Now, when we look at items or abilities that confer HP, we'll use 17 as the benchmark that signifies a level's worth of HP. For example, the unique helm Rockstopper grants 15 vitality (or 45 HP for a neutral character), worth 2.6 levels. Obviously, a character can't gain 0.6 levels, but the decimal portion is still useful as a measure.

There are a few important things to know about how LEQ works and what it means. The most important thing to know is that it doesn't actually measure overall character level improvement. Rather, LEQ measures how a certain aspect of a skill or piece of gear performs compared to character levels. If the character puts on a piece of gear with 34 HP, it's not the same as gaining two levels. It's simply that he gains the amount of HP that two levels would grant. Similarly, if a character gains eight levels' worth of damage output, he hasn't gained eight levels—he simply hits like a character eight levels higher. Gaining eight levels would involve gaining HP, hit rating, skill points, and so forth, all things that would be impossible to calculate at one time and which rarely all appear together on a single item. The other important thing to know about LEQ is that, sometimes, it can be highly contextual. An item that grants 34 HP always has an LEQ of two, but an item that grants a 10% bonus to HP has an LEQ that changes as the player's HP pool grows. As soon as the player's base HP exceeds 340, the item will have an LEQ of greater than two. Similarly, increases in things like DPS, elemental resistance, and damage reduction are all dependent on their context. An item that reduces all damage by 10 is extremely valuable at low levels because average damage doesn't exceed 10 by much. At higher levels, a 10% damage reduction is vastly more valuable because some of the endgame monsters (especially bosses) can do far more than 100 damage per strike. Because of this dynamic, I have performed all LEQ calculations using level-appropriate contexts for every item.

What Else Can an Item Do?

Gear causes accelerations by giving players more power than would ordinarily be appropriate for their level. Some of these ways are obvious. The one-handed club Felloak is a level three item, but it hits like a level 15 weapon, for an LEQ of 12. The beginning of the game is already easy, but if a low-level player equips Felloak while doing Tristram runs, they'll feel the acceleration. In a totally different manner, the String of Ears belt is a level 29 item that reduces magic damage received by 12 points. At that level, common enemies only do about 21 damage per spell, and so the damage reduction gives the player an effective HP bonus (vs magic) of more than 300 points, or almost 19 levels.

A Survey of Noteworthy Items, with LEQ

In this section, I'm going to highlight some items that are notable for their high LEQ values, as well as the variety of ways in which they achieve those values. Although there are a huge number of powerful items in the game, I have tried to focus on items that are powerful in orthogonal ways. I have also tried to highlight places where the LEQ system is insufficient or flawed. One proviso I need to make more generally is that the LEQ totals here are not equivalent to total levels gained. For example, an item that gives the player six LEQ of damage and eight LEQ of fire resistance would be rated at 14 LEQ. Nobody should make the mistake of thinking that this item makes the player 14 levels stronger. The total LEQ value is not an exact measurement that gets added to a player's character level. Think of it more as a brief summary of an item's various powers. What I'm highlighting is the way that *Diablo II* offers large amounts of power in a variety of ways. With this system, I'm analyzing the game's design, not trying to invent a way of assessing player gear for optimal play. No measurement system like this can ever be perfect, but tools like LEQ can still help us to understand game design if we understand its limitations.

(Note that the calculations for the rest of this subsection are all based on data obtained from The Arreat Summit—Items.)[74]

Weapons

Coldsteel Eye: Cutlass, 28 LEQ

This one-handed weapon is a good example of some fairly simple damage bonuses that can be measured in LEQ. At the first level the player can equip this, it already hits like a weapon 23 levels higher than it really is. Most of that is from a large damage modifier (225%). EAdd to this the "deadly strike" affix, which occasionally doubles damage, and this sword now hits like a weapon 28 levels higher than it actually is.

Stormspike: Stiletto, 62 LEQ

Elemental resistance can appear on any piece of gear, but it's less common on weapons than it is on armor. Stormspike offers 70 lightning resistance, which is worth about 42 levels of HP at the time the player can get this weapon. As I've said before, it's really only worth 42 LEQ against lightning, but lightning-enchanted enemies are one of the biggest nuisances in the game. Stormspike also hits like a weapon 20 levels higher than it actually is.

Spectral Shard: Blade, 10+ LEQ

Almost the opposite of Coldsteel Eye, this weapon actually hits for -11 LEQ (or, it hits like a magical weapon 11 levels lower than the best blue weapon of its type at the same level). But melee combat is not what this weapon is for. Instead, this weapon offers about 1.7 LEQ of resistance against all elements, and a great deal of an affix called "faster cast rate" (FCR). The latter affix can't be measured by LEQ because it depends on what spell the character is casting, but this item is one of the best sources for FCR in the game, and would boost spell DPS about 30%. This boost is, for virtually all offensive spells, a double-digit LEQ bonus.

The Jade Tan Do: Dagger, 216 LEQ*

Once I had done all the LEQ calculations, I noticed this item first when I sorted by highest LEQ. My calculations said it was worth a whopping 216 levels. This is misleading because although it offers a lot of damage and a lot of resistance, it's all in the poison element. Originally, the damage calculation yielded an LEQ of 70, but poison damage is spread out over time, and when converted to DPS, it comes out to about 14 LEQ instead. The item gains another 192 LEQ from poison resistance, but this is also misleading. Poison damage is one of the least common and least dangerous types of damage in the game. There are only two mandatory enemies in the game that put out large amounts of poison damage, so unless the player is fighting Andariel or Achmel the Cursed, this poison resistance is not as useful as the calculation indicates.

Lightsabre: Phase Blade, 70 LEQ

This weapon is a great example of benefits inflected for the level at which the player actually might find it. This item drops late in the game, at a point where enemies are sporting quite a bit of defense. Accordingly, it gains about 19 levels just because it ignores those enemies' defenses, which is an orthogonal perk. It also hits like a weapon 27 levels higher and offers moderate lightning resistance.

Azurewrath: Phase Blade, 1600 DPS Above Level 85

Like many complex rating systems that measure games (I'm looking at you, advanced baseball stats!), LEQ fails to accurately measure truly extreme cases. In this case, LEQ cannot measure the true value of the best unique sword in the game—Azurewrath—because there's nothing to compare it to. I can't compare Azurewrath to a magical weapon with a damage affix that's higher than level 85 because such an item doesn't exist. What I can say is that, compared to the maximum DPS available on a one-handed weapon, Azurewrath exceeds that amount by 1600. That's not 1600 damage per hit, that's 1600 damage per second, and that's before the game factors damage from abilities that multiply the damage of the weapon. Another reason why I examine this item is that the means of its power are interesting. Rather than having a single, outsized damage affix, Azurewrath has several different damage bonuses. There is a 250% direct damage affix, as well as several elemental damage affixes totaling 750 additional damage of several types. While these additional affixes don't incur multiplicative damage from skills, they are still useful because they will damage enemies who are immune to physical damage.

---

* LEQ measurement which is somewhat imprecise, because of damage over time elements, or the diminishing returns of hit rating.

Ume's Lament: Grim Wand, 12 LEQ

This necromancer weapon offers various direct bonuses to skill levels. Now, when it comes to the LEQ value of +skill affixes, the math portion is really easy; a +1 bonus to a specific skill (like Fireball) is equal to exactly one level of skill. That said, we can't just add up all the +skill affixes on an item and say that's the LEQ value because many of the modifiers are more complex than that. For example, Ume's Lament offers +2 to all necromancer skills. Does that mean the LEQ is two? No, because it affects all necromancer skills. The necromancer has more than 20 skills. Is the LEQ 40 or more? Again, no, because the Necromancer isn't actually going to use all of those skills directly. Instead, I value the "all skills" modifier at three LEQ per one point to all skills. The reason is that most builds in Diablo II rely primarily on three skills. Some builds rely on more, some builds rely on less, but most builds split the majority of their skill points between three primary skills, so the "+2 to all skills" modifier is worth six LEQ because it raises the level of three different skills by two points each.

Ume's Lament also has other modifiers, however. In addition to buffing all necromancer skills, it also buffs two specific skills: Terror and Decrepify. For cases like these, I had to manually audit skills in my spreadsheet. Both of these skills are necromancer curses. Enemies can only be under the effects of one curse at a time. Therefore, I value the bonuses at an LEQ of three (the bonus given to both of the curses), since the Necromancer will mostly be using just one of them, and certainly only one at a time. Is this valuation perfect? No, of course it isn't. There are some players who use four skills, and some who use five, and those players are often extremely proficient at *Diablo II*. This is not a theorycrafting text for optimal play; this is a design analysis that focuses on average player behavior, and most players spend most of their time using three skills.

Ume's Lament also gains three LEQ from a moderate mana bonus.

Beast: Runeword, 45 LEQ*

For the most part, I have not looked at runewords in this section—or anywhere else in the document. There are two reasons for this. First, runewords aren't that different from unique items in the things they can do. Many of the best runewords are considered to be the best item for the slot they occupy, but only because they do more things, not new things. The second problem with writing up the LEQ of runewords is that any weapon or item with the appropriate number of sockets can become a runeword, so there are no fixed stats. I've actually taken advantage of the variability problem for this write-up. Beast is such a high-level weapon that, like Azurewrath, there's nothing to compare its DPS to, so there's no way to perform an LEQ calculation for that part of the itemization. I therefore applied the stat boosts of the runeword to an inappropriately low-level mace, just so we can see how much power the runeword grants.

---

* LEQ measurement which is somewhat imprecise, because of damage over time elements, or the diminishing returns of hit rating.

Applied to a low-level item, Beast sits at about 45 LEQ, most of that coming from a large, direct damage affix (about 250% on average) plus a Fanaticism aura affix which adds another 186% direct damage, lots of attack speed, and a great deal of AR. The item gains about seven more LEQ from a combination of strength, energy, and Druid skills. I want to go back to that AR bonus from Fanaticism, though. Fanaticism at that level grants a percentage-based AR bonus. Like all percentage-based bonuses, it's way more valuable at high levels, so the LEQ of this affix would be much higher at the appropriate level. (But then we wouldn't be able to measure the LEQ of the DPS.)

Armor

Spirit Forge: Linked Mail, 12 LEQ

At level 35 (the first time you can equip it), this armor grants almost three levels of life. It also adds a surprising amount of fire damage, roughly equivalent to six levels. Then, it adds another three levels worth of strength. Finally, it has two sockets, which aren't even a factor in this equation since their value is so widely variable.

The fire damage is the most interesting part here. Fire damage is an example of what I call "off-slot" abilities. Typically, items equipped in the chest armor slot only gain defensive affixes. A few unique armor pieces, like this one, actually grant offensive affixes as well. This is a huge help for a defensively-minded character who is looking for a little extra punch. It is items like these that typify *Diablo II*. The right item can not only serve its primary purpose (like protecting the character), but can also make up for shortcomings in that player's weapon.

Iron Pelt: Trellised Armor, 263 LEQ

Thanks to a physical damage reduction of 10 (integer, not percent), this armor is worth more than 250 levels versus the physical damage of level-appropriate enemies. Enemies in level appropriate zones don't deal damage much above 10, so almost all the damage is mitigated. As the game goes on and enemies deal more damage, the value of this item decays precipitously. For a level-appropriate zone, or as part of a set of items which all have physical damage reduction, it's a very powerful piece of gear.

The Spirit Shroud: Ghost Armor, 13 LEQ

This item does for magic damage what Iron Pelt does for physical damage. The items drop from enemies of a similar level. The big difference is that magic damage is less common, but usually hits harder. Thus, the LEQ on this item is lower, despite the roughly equal reduction in absolute damage. More damage makes it through this item and hits the player.

Steel Carapace: Shadow Plate, 36 LEQ

An item for the defense-obsessed, this armor grants 50% resistance to cold (27 LEQ, as level-appropriate enemies deal a lot of damage), as well as 11 points of absolute damage reduction versus physical types (nine LEQ). This is another good example of an item whose LEQ is a little tricky. The cold resist and physical reduction can't overlap. No attack is both physical and cold-based, although there are some attacks that deal both types separately. Is it fair to assess this item as the sum of its parts? In the strictest sense, no. At the same time, however, the high LEQ of this item still shows us its versatility, which is still extremely valuable.

Thundergod's Vigor: War Belt, 24 LEQ

This item has a great variety of buffs, including good lightning resistance (14 LEQ), as well as HP and strength (7.5 LEQ combined). This item also has some good off-slot perks. It's rare to get strength on a belt, and even rarer to get so much of it. While strength isn't a stat most players seek, it's useful when it appears on an item that also has more important stats as well. Having a large strength bonus on a belt also allows the player to meet strength requirements on heavier items in slots like armor or weapons.

Bloodfist: Heavy Gloves, 7 LEQ

Although the planned deficits of the last difficulty make super-powered weapons necessary, there are still plenty of powerful unique items at low levels that can give the player an acceleration. Bloodfist offers five levels of direct damage enhancement. Although damage modifiers often appear on rings, amulets and weapons, it's rare for them to appear on gloves. Bloodfist offers this perk in act one of the first difficulty, and the player can find it in their very first play session.

Dracul's Grasp: Vampirebone Gloves, LEQ

These gloves are difficult to assess through LEQ because they have some incomparable attributes. Firstly, they offer high amounts of lifesteal, which transfers HP to the striker on every hit. This expands the effective HP pool for attacking characters but can't be measured in LEQ because there's no base amount of lifesteal per level. If we could measure it, however, the LEQ for this item would be quite high because in addition to having lifesteal built into the item, the gloves also have a chance to cast the necromancer curse "Life Tap" when striking the enemy, which grants even more lifesteal. This is a good example of an "off-class" ability, in which an item gives any fighter class—Barbarians, Assassins, etc—the ability to use a highly beneficial Necromancer curse. Many of the best items have off-class abilities. Some items (like the Trang-Oul's set) simply allow a new class to cast some other class's spell. Some of these off-class abilities are performed on strike, or when struck. They're often quite useful and can solve problems like a lack of appropriate elemental damage.

Crown of Thieves: Grand Crown, 21 LEQ

This helm is worth 21 levels in LEQ, gaining most of that value from significant sources of dexterity, health, and mana. These are useful for virtually anyone who uses a weapon or a shield. The wearer also gains another 10 levels of LEQ against fire damage. The nice thing about this item is that although it doesn't give any one outstanding bonus that we can measure, it offers a variety of moderate bonuses.

Additionally, it also offers significant lifesteal which cannot be measured, but which is quite useful for many classes.

Veil of Steel: Spired Helm, 42 LEQ

This helm gains nearly 40 LEQ from a combination of moderate strength, moderate HP, and a huge amount of resistance against all elements. If anything, LEQ underestimates the value of this item, since resistance LEQ values are the one place where I don't add up LEQ in the summary. Instead, I simply use the highest resistance's LEQ as being indicative of the resistance overall. If we were to measure the combined LEQ of the resistances, the helm's LEQ would be closer to 140.

Chains of Honor: Runeword, 72 LEQ

Similar to the Crown of Thieves, this runeword armor provides a variety of benefits that could be used by many different builds. It draws most of its LEQ from 65% elemental resistance, but also offers physical resistance, lifesteal, strength, and even 25% magic find. The strength and lifesteal benefit weapon-users more than casters, but the armor also has a +2 to all skills modifier. On top of the copious resistances and magic find, this is an item any class would covet.

Influencing Both Sides of the R/T Ratio

All of the items in the previous section do a great job of decreasing the time component of the R/T ratio by giving the player a huge increase in power. With items that can boost a given stat by more than 50 levels, the player will have a much easier time disposing of hordes of monsters rapidly. The real pleasure of unique items in *Diablo II* is that many of the same items that cut down on the time denominator in the R/T ratio also boost the reward numerator. The most famous example is the magic find affix, which gives the player a better chance of finding magic, rare, set, and unique items, but there are actually several items that also increase either gold (which, admittedly, isn't very useful) or even experience points. Some of the best items in the game are the ones that are powerful enough to cut down the time component while also driving up the reward. I'm going to look at a couple of these items below. There are many others that I don't list, but the two below are illustrative of the design idea.

Skullder's Ire: Russet Armor, 7 LEQ

Although not tremendously powerful by itself, Skullder's Ire also sports a scaling magic-find affix that can scale as high as 123% increased odds of finding magic items. It also sports a +1 to All Skill affix, which makes the item ideal for ranged characters who don't desperately need HP or armor.

Harlequin Crest: Shako, 30 LEQ

Perhaps the most popular unique item in the game, this helm offers +2 to all skills, as well as HP and mana bonuses that scale with player level. On top of all of that, the helm offers a 50% magic-find bonus, which helps the player to earn more elite gear as they go.

From Schaefer Variation to Acceleration Flow

As we have seen throughout Chapter 3 of this book, accelerations and decelerations are an important (and idiosyncratic) design feature of *Diablo II*. I want to stop for a moment and deal with the psychology of accelerations more generally. I call the peculiar euphoria of accelerations acceleration flow. It is a natural psychological phenomenon that occurs in RPGs, even those that lack Schaefer variation or any similar structure. I'll describe the phenomenon of acceleration flow in the following section, but the thing we have to know is that Schaefer variation produces acceleration incidentally. During my interviews with the developers of *Diablo II*, they all said that they like the idea of acceleration flow, and they all recognized that it was happening, but it wasn't something they planned for.[75-77] (I don't want to give the illusion that any of them used my term, or any other term, for acceleration flow. I merely described the phenomenon and they agreed they had observed some form of it.)

Acceleration flow is best explained by a famous (and anachronistic) example: the endgame content in *World of Warcraft*. Once a character in *World of Warcraft* hits the current maximum level, he or she can join high-level "raids" that offer the game's most powerful gear. This dynamic, however, brings up an interesting question. There is no higher level of content than raids. What is all that gear for, then? The answer is that the gear exists to start an acceleration. To get raid gear, the player needs to kill raid bosses. Those bosses tend to be very difficult to kill for a variety of reasons, but one thing that makes them easier is having better gear. Thus begins a positive feedback loop. Every time a raid boss falls, it drops high-end gear. Each piece of high-end gear makes the next raid boss easier. (This is rather like the accelerations we've already discussed.) Not only does the player acquire more and more power, but the rate at which they acquire power accelerates as well. This rapid increase in power, after struggling all the way to max level, gives the player a euphoric feeling of accomplishment. That feeling is acceleration flow. The psychological phenomenon is analogous to the phenomenon made famous by the Hungarian researcher Mihaly Csikczentmihalyi. When someone is in a "flow state," they're completely focused and engaged by whatever they're doing. They don't notice the passage of time, or anything going on around them. Someone in the thrall of acceleration flow is experiencing something similar. They can endlessly repeat the same maneuvers against the same bosses (even though everything is rote by now) because they're not thinking about the mindless repetitions. Rather, they're thinking about how powerful their character is growing, and wondering where the ceiling to that power might be.

Before acceleration flow can happen, the designers have to establish a baseline, or else the players can't tell that they're accelerating away from it. This baseline is what I call the median level progression rate, or MLPR.

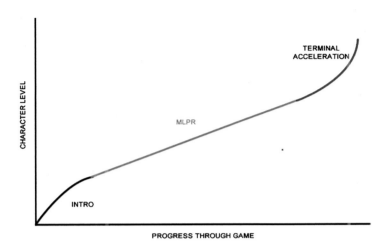

For most of any RPG, player characters gain levels at a fairly consistent rate. In some RPGs, like *World of Warcraft*, *Disgaea*, or most of the *Final Fantasies* after 6, the player is then able to greatly accelerate the rate at which they're able to gain power. This usually happens at the end of the game in what I call a *terminal acceleration*, which helps to make the end of those games feel more climactic. Occasionally, these games will also build in a smaller, mid-game acceleration (*FF6's Floating Continent*, *Chrono Trigger's Magus Castle*) meant to embellish the tension of an important plot point. These accelerations are smaller and not nearly as common as terminal accelerations.

It's important to know that the concept of the MLPR is a theoretical one. It's useful as a framework for understanding accelerations, but not as a precise mathematical datum. Technically every game does have a literal median R/T ratio, although it would be hard to figure out exactly what it is. Most players will get used to the idea that level-ups occur at a certain rate, however, and they will sense large deviations (accelerations or decelerations) from that rate. In many games, especially multiplayer RPGs, the MLPR is sectional. That is, a game like *World of Warcraft* or *Diablo II* will break down into discrete sections, and the player will understand that each of those sections will have its own MLPR. In *Diablo II*, those sections are fairly obvious: each difficulty setting has its own MLPR. As players progress through the difficulty settings, they'll quickly notice that the R/T ratio has changed permanently. Very attentive players will also notice a smaller change in the R/T ratio across each act. Visualized, the MLPR of *Diablo II* would look something like what you see in the graph below.

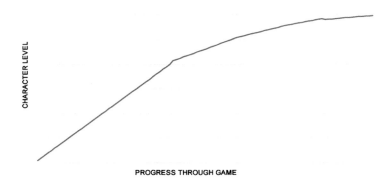

CHARACTER LEVEL

PROGRESS THROUGH GAME

Overall this gives the player an impression of an R/T ratio that arcs downwards across the course of the game. This arc is an important one for the extreme late-game accelerations that *Diablo II* affords the player.

Because the sectional MLPR slowly arcs downward across the course of the game, it gives the player a clear benchmark for power, and allows for even steeper accelerations. The early-game MLPR, in which the player can kill most regular creatures in one hit and gain levels several times an hour, serves as a great benchmark for players. Although players will naturally accept that the late-game is slower and more difficult, they never forget how easy things once were. Thus, when the player begins to acquire powerful gear and top-level skills in the later game, they have a very clear benchmark against which to measure. Are enemies falling as fast as they did in the beginning of the game—even though the player-character is now level 65? This is an important part of the feeling of acceleration flow. The player will feel the acceleration more acutely if they have a clear frame of reference against which they can measure the acceleration. Because the sectional MLPR declines over time, the player can get even greater euphoria than if it were steadier.

When buffed by numerous +skill affixes, some of the higher-level spells like Frozen Orb, Blessed Hammer, and Lightning Fury can actually kill whole screens full of enemies, raising the player's kill rate (and thus EXP/gear rate) above even the early game MLPR. This acceleration doesn't always last, but it's a terrific feeling while the player is in it, and a great example of the phenomenon as a whole.

The EXP/Gear Crossover

After level 75, *Diablo II* characters incur diminishing returns on all earned EXP. This seems like a roadblock to accelerations, but it's really just a transition from one type of reward to another—and in any case, it can be overcome by brute force. The goal of the EXP penalty, according to David Brevik,[78] is to make the game longer and to change the focus of high-level players from EXP to elite gear.

Given how powerful some of the end-game gear is, this makes a lot of sense. At level 80, it often takes equally long for a player to gain one character level or farm bosses for one piece of high-end gear (depending on magic find and luck). The gear is usually far more valuable than the character level, anyway. At high levels, a player can easily find a gear with LEQs of 10 or higher in several stats. While EXP penalties drive down the experience component of the R/T ratio, the increasing potential for gear (and the player's extreme power driving down the time component) allows for a big terminal acceleration.

Looking at Terminal Accelerations

After the EXP/gear crossover, players who continue developing their character will enter the terminal acceleration. Whether the player intends to get his or her character to level 99 or simply to find a certain set of gear, the terminal acceleration is the organizing principle of end-game content. In other RPGs, the driving force behind end-game content is to beat the last boss or an optional boss. In *Diablo II*, the player might beat the last boss dozens, hundreds, or even thousands of times in a process called "Baal runs." In that context, killing the last boss isn't terribly significant. Instead, the terminal acceleration provides structure for the player's activities instead. For experienced *Diablo II* players, this is where the real game begins. Many other players stop the game at this point, however, because the rate at which the player gains character levels has dropped precipitously. Without that clear benchmark, some players can't tell that they're making progress. Given how high the LEQ values are for items in the endgame, however, players really do gain power when they acquire new items—much more power than they were gaining earlier in the game. The process isn't quite as smooth or regular as it was before character level 75.

One of the most important dynamics in the terminal acceleration is the way that set randomness affects the R/T ratio. At the end of the game, the player starts to see some of the best gear available, but the order in which he or she receives that gear is random. A player just entering the end-game needs a weapon, armor, a helm, a belt, boots, gloves, two rings, and an amulet (and maybe a shield). We can think of this as a set with many potential pieces. At first, any high-level item will be an upgrade, because the player needs a new item for every gear slot. There are nine slots to fill, but any high-level drop will upgrade one of them. If the player gets a belt, a helm, a weapon, a ring, and boots, then the odds of finding an upgrade drop below 50% because the player has already filled five of nine slots. (This assumes that items from every slot drop at roughly equal rates. This isn't true for every set, but the overall principle holds true.) The same dynamic is repeated for groups. Let's say we have a group of five players farming Baal, and they're looking for the following items:

Thundergod's Vigor
Gore Riders
Homunculus

Immortal King's Forge
Immortal King's Detail
Immortal King's Pillar

These aren't the only items in Baal's loot lists on the highest difficulty setting—
there are hundreds more. For the sake of this example, let's say there are 60. Our
hypothetical group is looking for six items, so the odds of getting a specific item
from this list are low (1/60), but the odds of getting any of the items are much
higher (1/10). Let's visualize it in terms of R/T.

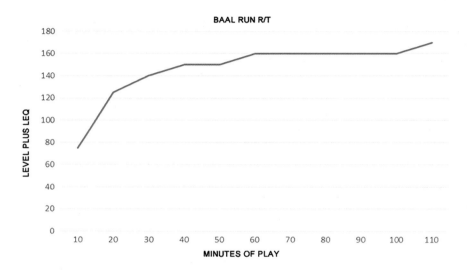

Because the power of the endgame rewards is so high, it softens the return to the
MLPR. When the acceleration finally ends, most players are essentially done with
the game.

The True Power of Sets

Any combination of several pieces of gear can form a set. Many builds call for a
specific group of unique items and runewords whose effects are synergetic in a
way that is greater than the sum of their parts. In *Diablo II* there are also what
we might call "diegetic" or "denoted" sets—gear which the game explicitly marks
as sets. Outfits like Sigon's Complete Steel, Natalya's Odium, and Tal Rasha's
Wrappings gain special bonuses as the set increases in completeness. Set gear is
only slightly more common than unique gear, and so often useful by itself, but
as the set bonuses start to mount, there are clear inflection points in the LEQ of
the set as a whole.

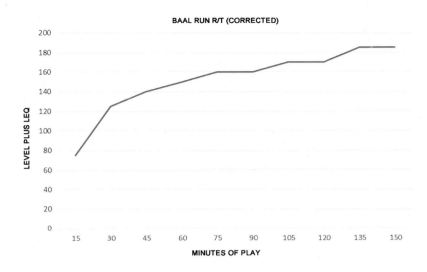

BAAL RUN R/T (CORRECTED)

The rewards for completing a set are commensurate with the time and effort it takes to do so. On a piece by piece basis, unique and runeword gear is more powerful than most sets. The most powerful build for most classes involves many non-set items. Through explicit set items, however, the *Diablo* designers give the player a window into how set randomness works and add extra incentive to pursue complete sets and the accelerations they can provide.

The Other Side of Terminal Accelerations

One of the most illuminating things that David Brevik told me during our interview was that the extraneous gear players get during the terminal acceleration period is actually intentional.[79] He explained that when a Sorceress sees an incredible Barbarian item drop, or an Assassin finds the game's best Druid helm, the player is supposed to save that item to make a new character. (How the notion of shared items can be reconciled with the character-specific item stashes is anyone's guess.) This one idea brings together the game's roguelike heritage, character classes and acceleration-based gameplay. The most essential experience of the roguelike is starting the game over again. One of the pillars of the tabletop RPG is its different character classes. The hallmark of *Diablo II* is its acceleration-based gameplay. Starting the game over with a new character class that already has a bunch of powerful gear (which causes an acceleration) ties all three of these ideas together and extends the playing time of the game in an idiosyncratic way. For me, the impetus to restart as new characters is the encapsulation of everything that makes *Diablo II* elegant, from a game design perspective. It results in an incredible synthesis of all of the game's influences into one long, engaging loop.

4

Conclusion
Lessons from Diablo II

At the end of every *Reverse Design*, I summarize the major lessons of the book. I want to be clear that I do not believe that the lessons of videogame design can be broken down into rules of thumb. One of the overarching themes in this series has been that execution is far more important than theoretical ideas. The point of the *Reverse Design* series is to provide extensive detail about how the great games executed their ideas, in particular detail, from beginning to end. Inasmuch as books like these do need endings, a summary of the lessons seems useful enough.

1. A great variety of videogames, *Diablo II* included, mix ideas from different genres that came before them. *Diablo II* borrows from roguelikes, traditional tabletop RPGs, and console action games. Sometimes it reuses an idea wholesale: maps and item drops in *Diablo II* are very close to those in their immediate ancestors, *Moria* and *Angband*. Some ideas are modified: permadeath is optional, but all players lose experience and gold when they die. The same is true with character classes; every class plays differently, but they don't follow the traditional roles of the tabletop. In

other words, *Diablo II* picks and chooses which ideas will work for it, which won't work, and which just need a little adaptation.

2. There are many different ways to look at randomness in game design. All randomness might be mathematically similar, but most players (and the designers who seek to entertain them) don't perceive the complex mathematics. Instead, it's useful to use different lenses to look at randomness from a psychological perspective. Different systems in *Diablo* operate by set randomness, randomness within a range, deck-of-cards randomness, and slice-of-pie randomness. If you're implementing a procedural system in your game, try prototyping it by using a deck of cards, a pie graph, or a bag of *Scrabble* tiles to which you assign special values.

3. Remember that if you're going to rely heavily on randomness through procedural generation, the game will have a very "copy/paste" feel if you don't have enough cards in the deck or tiles in the bag. Remember that the component presets in the procedurally generated maps of *Diablo II* required the full-time work of three people for several years to feel as "random" as they are.

4. The fundamental design structure of console action games, Nishikado motion, has been amazingly durable across the history of videogames. Even in genres where it isn't necessary (like stat-heavy RPGs), it can be a useful way to keep your game from being too easy or too frustrating. Remember that no game is ever perfectly balanced!

5. If you're trying to emulate Nishikado motion, your game is going to need gear and enemies that are sometimes inappropriately strong for the area where they appear.

6. If you want help balancing your gear, try using LEQ. It's not a perfect metric; there is no perfect metric! But if you're designing an RPG, it's useful to think of all power in the context of character levels since you're going to have them in the game anyway.

7. Anticipate the possibility of accelerations, and use them in the right places in your game. The prevailing wisdom about RPGs is that the need for grinding in a game will repel large parts of the audience. *Diablo II* relies heavily on players repeating the same content over and over in order to farm EXP and gear, and yet it is one of the most popular RPGs of all time. That's because acceleration flow turns otherwise boring repetition into an exciting process of exponential growth.

References

Note: Three of the interviews cited here (Brevik, Hedlund, and Scandizzo) were done during the writing of this book. The interview with Max Schaefer was much older, from 2012. I interviewed him while working on a totally different project, but his comments about the difficulty structure in *Diablo II* and *Torchlight* (being like a "sine wave") led to the thesis of this book many years later.

1. Gygax, Gary. The Player's Handbook. TSR Games, 1977.
2. Gygax, Gary. Monster Manual. TSR Games, 1977.
3. Gygax, Gary. The Dungeon Master's Guide. TSR Games, 1979.
4. Scandizzo, Stefan. Interview, March 4, 2017.
5. Brevik, David. Interview, January 25, 2017.
6. ibid.
7. Schaefer, Max. Interview, October 15, 2012.
8. The Arreat Summit. "Classes." http://classic.battle.net/diablo2exp/classes/.
9. Clarke, Chris. "To Hit Calculations." http://www.chrisclarke.co.uk/D2stuff/PDFs/ToHit.htm.
10. ibid.
11. ibid.
12. ibid.
13. Diablo Wiki. "Blocking." https://diablo2.diablowiki.net/Block.
14. ibid.
15. The Arreat Summit. "Skills." http://classic.battle.net/diablo2exp/skills/.
16. ibid.
17. The Arreat Summit. "Monsters." http://classic.battle.net/diablo2exp/monsters/.
18. The Arreat Summit. "Skills." http://classic.battle.net/diablo2exp/skills/.
19. The Arreat Summit. "Items." http://classic.battle.net/diablo2exp/items/.

20. The Arreat Summit. "Skills." http://classic.battle.net/diablo2exp/skills/.
21. ibid.
22. Diablo II Attack Speed Calculator. http://diablo3.ingame.de/diablo-2/calculatoren/angriffsgeschwindigkeit/.
23. Brevik, David. Interview, January 25, 2017.
24. The Arreat Summit. "Skills." http://classic.battle.net/diablo2exp/skills/.
25. Vertical Slice. "S03E18: Graybeard Games' David Brevik." https://www.youtube.com/watch?v=WUqWtNs64nk.
26. Hedlund, Steig. Interview, March 7, 2017.
27. Brevik, David. Interview, January 25, 2017.
28. Diablo Wiki. "Move Speed." http://diablo.wikia.com/wiki/Movement_speed.
29. Brevik, David. Interview, January 25, 2017.
30. Hedlund, Steig. Interview, March 7, 2017.
31. Diablo Wiki. "Affixes." https://diablo.gamepedia.com/Affixes_(Diablo_II)#.2BElemental_Damage.
32. The Arreat Summit. "Monsters." http://classic.battle.net/diablo2exp/monsters/.
33. ibid.
34. The Arreat Summit. "Items." http://classic.battle.net/diablo2exp/items.
35. The Arreat Summit. "Items." http://classic.battle.net/diablo2exp/items.
36. Scandizzo, Stefan. Interview, March 4, 2017.
37. Brevik, David. Interview, January 25, 2017.
38. Hedlund, Steig. Interview, March 7, 2017.
39. Diabloiinet. "Nodrop Tables." https://www.diabloii.net/forums/threads/no-drop-tables.741117/.
40. Diablo Wiki. "Treasure Classes 1.10." https://diablo2.diablowiki.net/TC_1.10.
41. Fenriradramelk. "Magic Find Mechanics Guide." https://www.gamefaqs.com/pc/197113-diablo-ii/faqs/55871.
42. ibid.
43. Diablo Wiki. "Treasure Classes 1.10." https://diablo2.diablowiki.net/TC_1.10.
44. ibid.
45. ibid.
46. Brevik, David. Interview, January 25, 2017.
47. Diablo Wiki. "Magic Find Percentages." https://diablo2.diablowiki.net/Magic_Find#Magic_Find_Percentages.
48. Diablo Wiki. "Magic Find Diminishing Returns." https://diablo2.diablowiki.net/Magic_find_diminishing_returns.
49. Scandizzo, Stefan. Interview, March 4, 2017.
50. ibid.
51. ibid.
52. ibid.
53. Hedlund, Steig. Interview, March 7, 2017.
54. Scandizzo, Stefan. Interview, March 4, 2017.
55. Brevik, David. Interview, January 25, 2017.

56. Diablo Wiki. "Area Level." https://diablo2.diablowiki.net/Area_Level.

57. The Arreat Summit. "Monsters." http://classic.battle.net/diablo2exp/monsters/.

58. ibid.

59. The Arreat Summit. "Experience." http://classic.battle.net/diablo2exp/basics/experience.shtml.

60. The Arreat Summit. "Monsters." http://classic.battle.net/diablo2exp/monsters/.

61. The Arreat Summit. "Items." http://classic.battle.net/diablo2exp/items/.

62. ibid.

63. Diablo Wiki. "Affixes." https://diablo.gamepedia.com/Affixes_(Diablo_II)#.2BElemental_Damage.

64. The Arreat Summit. "Skills." http://classic.battle.net/diablo2exp/skills/.

65. Clarke, Chris. "To Hit Calculations." http://www.chrisclarke.co.uk/D2stuff/PDFs/ToHit.htm.

66. The Arreat Summit. "Items." http://classic.battle.net/diablo2exp/items/.

67. Diablo Wiki. "Affixes." https://diablo.gamepedia.com/Affixes_(Diablo_II)#.2BElemental_Damage.

68. The Arreat Summit. "Monsters." http://classic.battle.net/diablo2exp/monsters/.

69. Clarke, Chris. "To Hit Calculations." http://www.chrisclarke.co.uk/D2stuff/PDFs/ToHit.htm.

70. The Arreat Summit. "Classes." http://classic.battle.net/diablo2exp/classes/.

71. Diablo Wiki. "Affixes." https://diablo.gamepedia.com/Affixes_(Diablo_II)#.2BElemental_Damage.

72. The Arreat Summit. "Monsters." http://classic.battle.net/diablo2exp/monsters/.

73. ibid.

74. The Arreat Summit. "Items." http://classic.battle.net/diablo2exp/items/.

75. Schaefer, Max. Interview, October 15, 2012.

76. Brevik, David. Interview, January 25, 2017.

77. Hedlund, Steig. Interview, March 7, 2017.

78. Brevik, David. Interview, January 25, 2017.

79. ibid.

Index

C